Augustinian Just War Theory and the Wars in Afghanistan and Iraq

PETER LANG
New York • Washington, D.C./Baltimore • Bern
Frankfurt • Berlin • Brussels • Vienna • Oxford

Augustinian Just War Theory and the Wars in Afghanistan and Iraq

Confessions, Contentions, and the Lust for Power

Edited by Craig J. N. de Paulo,
Patrick A. Messina, & Daniel P. Tompkins

PETER LANG
New York • Washington, D.C./Baltimore • Bern
Frankfurt • Berlin • Brussels • Vienna • Oxford

Library of Congress Cataloging-in-Publication Data

Augustinian just war theory and the wars in Afghanistan and Iraq:
confessions, contentions, and the lust for power / edited by
Craig J. N. de Paulo, Patrick A. Messina, Daniel P. Tompkins.
p. cm.
Includes bibliographical references.
1. War—Religious aspects—Christianity. 2. Just war doctrine.
3. United States—Foreign relations—Moral and ethical aspects. 4. Christianity
and international relations—United States. 5. Afghan War, 2001– —Moral
and ethical aspects. 6. Iraq War, 2003– —Moral and ethical aspects.
7. United States—Military policy—Moral and ethical aspects.
8. United States—Military policy—Religious aspects. 9. Augustine,
Saint, Bishop of Hippo. I. De Paulo, Craig J. N.
II. Messina, Patrick A. III. Tompkins, Daniel P.
BT736.2A84   261.8'73—dc23   2011017364
ISBN 978-1-4331-1232-4

Bibliographic information published by **Die Deutsche Nationalbibliothek**.
Die Deutsche Nationalbibliothek lists this publication in the "Deutsche
Nationalbibliografie"; detailed bibliographic data is available
on the Internet at http://dnb.d-nb.de/.

FSC
Mixed Sources
product group from well-managed
forests, controlled sources and
recycled wood or fiber

Cert no. SCS-COC-002464
www.fsc.org
©1996 Forest Stewardship Council

Cover art: *Guernica* by Pablo Picasso © 2011 Estate of Pablo Picasso /
Artists Rights Society (ARS), New York

The paper in this book meets the guidelines for permanence and durability
of the Committee on Production Guidelines for Book Longevity
of the Council of Library Resources.

© 2011 Peter Lang Publishing, Inc., New York
29 Broadway, 18th floor, New York, NY 10006
www.peterlang.com

Printed in the United States of America

In memoriam
Pope John Paul II

Contents

Acknowledgments

F irst of all, we are delighted and honored to acknowledge our sincere gratitude to His Eminence, The Most Rev. Seán Cardinal O' Malley, O.F.M. Cap., the Roman Catholic Archbishop of Boston, for graciously writing the Preface to this volume.

With sincere gratitude, we are also deeply honored and very indebted to the Rev. Dr. Roland J. Teske, S. J., Donald J. Schuenke Professor Emeritus of Philosophy at Marquette University, for graciously writing the Foreword to this volume.

We are also very indebted to our distinguished contributors, including Professor John D. Caputo, David R. Cook Chair Emeritus of Philosophy at Villanova University and Thomas J. Watson Professor of Philosophy, Religion and Humanities at Syracuse University, Professor Dieter Blumenwitz, Professor of International Law at the Ukrainian Free University in Munich, Germany, His late Eminence, Avery Cardinal Dulles, S.J., formerly the Laurence J. McGinley Professor of Religion and Society at Fordham University, Dr. Joseph H. Hagan, President Emeritus of Assumption College, Colonel Jack Jacobs, U.S.A. Ret.'d., MSNBC Military Analyst, Professor Brian Kane, Chair and Professor of Philosophy and Theology at De Sales University, Professor Joseph Margolis, Laura H. Carnell Professor of Philosophy at Temple University, The Hon. George J. Marlin, former Executive Director of the Port Authority of New York and New Jersey, The Hon. Thomas Melady, former U. S. Ambassador to the Holy See, His Excellency, The Most Rev. Edwin O' Brien, Archbishop of Baltimore and Archbishop Emeritus of the U. S. Military Archdiocese, and Professor Frederick Van Fleteren, Professor of Philosophy at La Salle University.

Much gratitude is due to Professor Bernhardt Blumenthal, Chair of the Foreign Language Department and Director of the graduate program in Central and Eastern European Studies at La Salle University in Philadelphia, for his gracious assistance in translating Professor Blumenwitz's chapter into English from the original German, and also to Professor Nicholas Rudnytzky for all of his kind assistance. We would also like to extend our gratitude to Professor Leonid Rudnytzky, Professor Emeritus of Slavic Languages at La Salle University and Rector Emeritus of the Ukrainian Free University in Munich, for all of his gracious assistance and many suggestions. We are grateful to the Rev. Dr. William J. Geisler for all of his insightful comments and recommendations.

We are delighted to thank Mr. Frank Giordano, then President of the Union League of Philadelphia, for all of his graciousness and hospitality in hosting our events at the prestigious Union League of Philadelphia. We are also very grateful to acknowledge the support and encouragement of Col. William P. Boswell, U.S.A.F. (Ret'd.), who greatly assisted us in raising funds for the symposium we organized at the Union League of Philadelphia.

We are equally delighted to acknowledge our sincere gratitude to Dr. Wayne Huss, Professor of History and Chair of the Division of Humanities at Gwynedd Mercy College, for his generous support with our scholarly endeavors. We would also like to thank Dr. Lisa McGarry, Interim Dean of the School of Arts and Sciences at Gwynedd Mercy College, for her gracious support. Finally, we must also acknowledge the kindness of Dr. Kathleen Owens, President of Gwynedd Mercy College, and Dr. Robert Funk, Acting Vice President for Academic Affairs at the College.

Many thanks are also due to Professor de Paulo's former research assistant, Mr. Walter G. Kealey, III, who was invaluable in assisting us with the research for this volume, and to Mr. Andrew Thompson, who assisted in transcribing the text of the first symposium for Chapter One of this volume.

It should also be mentioned that all of the statements that appear in our book from the two respective symposia on the topic of just war theory were taken by professional stenographers, and these discussions were notarized and certified by Strehlow & Associates, a court reporting agency, of Newtown, Pennsylvania, who provided these services. The statements have been edited only for clarity without any change in content. The symposium recorded in Chapter Two of this book was transcribed by Ms. Beth A. McKenna. The symposium recorded in Chapter Three was transcribed by Ms. Shauna Detty.

We are especially grateful to Mrs. Catherine Conroy de Paulo, Lecturer in English at Pennsylvania State University, for her many hours of gracious assistance with the proofreading and copyediting of this volume.

Preface

Most Rev. Seán Cardinal O'Malley, O.F.M. Cap.
Archbishop of Boston

P lease allow me this opportunity to express my gratitude to Drs. Craig J. N. de Paulo, Patrick Messina and Daniel Tompkins who have edited, *Augustinian Just War Theory and the Wars in Afghanistan and Iraq: Confessions, Contentions and the Lust for Power*. This volume comes at a time when many followers of Christ question the war and the role of the Church. The following pages present in a clear fashion the complex issues that surround this international concern for peace and justice in our world. The contributions by numerous distinguished intellects along with experts on what constitutes a just war will navigate the reader with a clearer understanding.

This volume is dedicated *in memoriam* to His Holiness, Pope John Paul II. As a young man in Poland, Pope John Paul II witnessed first hand the devastation of war among humanity. Truly, the pope was a peacemaker. As one of the great leaders of our time, the Holy Father helped to define during his papacy what is the definition of just war. Above all, he reinforced that the direction during an international dispute between nations must be directed towards the dignity of the human person. Thus, the need to protect the innocent must always be the main focus.

I am sure you join with me in prayer that the daily disputes in Afghanistan and Iraq will be solved without further bloodshed. One of the titles associated with Jesus Christ is Prince of Peace.

May his peace be with those entrusted with leadership so that all will unite together that peace and justice may reign.

Foreword

Roland J. Teske, S.J.
Donald J. Scheunke Professor Emeritus of Philosophy
Marquette University

W hen we studied in moral theology the conditions for a just war in the mid-60's at the time of the Cuban missile crisis, most of my peers and I in the seminary were struck by the fact that, while the principles given for waging a just war seemed solidly reasonable, they seemed somewhat inapplicable in the atomic age, where whole cities could be taken out by a single bomb or missile. The principles in our moral theology text gave five conditions for a just war: that war must be declared by legitimate authority, that it must have a just cause, that it must be the only means to the goal, that war be waged with the preservation of its due manner, and that the war be limited to obtaining just reparation and just conditions of peace. Further conditions required that there be some hope of victory, that far greater evils than goods were not foreseen to be the result of victory, and that it not result in greater harm to the true religion. It is hard to imagine how President Kennedy might have used these principles in the face of the threat of Russian missiles being fired at the United States from Cuba. Recent conflicts following the disasters of September 11, 2001 have made the application of the traditional conditions for a just war even more challenging and difficult.

For much of the past thirty some years I have devoted most of my academic life to the life and works of Augustine of Hippo, who, as everyone knows, was the author of the just-war theory. But as with so many of those things that everyone knows, this one has always seemed a bit shaky to me, even after I had translated eleven volumes of his works into English and read many others. Somehow I never found anything that seemed to amount to a just-war theory. In fact, in one of his early dialogues, *On the Free Choice of the Will* (*De libero arbitrio*), there is a passage that would seem to preclude any killing of another human being, even in self-defense. In speaking of killing another human being in defense of one's life or chastity, Evodius says: "Hence, I certainly do not find fault with the law that permits such people to be killed, but I do not find any way to defend those who kill them." And Augustine replies: "Much less do I find why you seek a defense for men whom no law holds guilty." But then Evodius wonders whether what temporal law permits is not forbidden by eternal law and says, "It seems to me that this law that is written for governing a people rightly permits these things and that the divine law punishes them."[1] Hence, in the early part of this early work written before his ordination as a priest, Augustine held that killing even in self-defense was perhaps permissible under temporal law, but still punishable and therefore forbidden and wrong under divine law. Such a principle would seem to undermine any attempt to justify killing in self-defense, not to mention to justify war in self-defense, at least in the eyes of God.

Quite different is the bishop of Hippo's view in Letter 189 to Boniface, a Christian general, the tribune of Africa, who would later become the count of Africa. The letter was written in approximately 417 over twenty years after Augustine's consecration as bishop of Hippo. After exhorting Boniface about the importance of love for God and one's neighbor, Augustine tells him that he should "not suppose that no one can please God who as a soldier carries the weapons of war." He gives examples of David from the Old Testament and of Cornelius the centurion from the New Testament and cites the teaching of John the Baptist to soldiers who came to him for baptism. Augustine points out that while some Christians fight against invisible enemies, Boniface fights against the visible barbarians. He reminds Boniface that, when he takes up arms, he should be thankful to God for his physical strength and aim at peace. "Only necessity requires war in order that God may set us free from necessity and preserve us in peace. For we do not seek peace in order to stir up war, but we wage war in order to acquire peace." He tells Boniface to "be a peacemaker even in war in order that by conquering you might bring to the benefit of peace those whom you fight." He urges that necessity and not desire should be the cause of slaying the enemy in battle and argues that mercy is owed to those who have been defeated or captured. Augustine then turns to the battle for marital chastity, with which Boniface had his own problems, and he says nothing more about war against the barbarian enemy.[2]

Augustine also dealt with the topic of war in his *Answer to Faustus, a Manichaean* (*Contra Faustum Manichaeum*) written between 408 and 410 in answer to the Manichaean bishop, who had written his *Chapters*, against a convert to the Catholic Church from Manichaeism, perhaps against Augustine himself who was certainly the most prominent of such converts. Faustus had, as a good Manichaean, attacked the Old Testament for many reasons, among which he included Abraham's readiness to sacrifice his son and the wars waged by Moses. In the twenty-second book of the work, which runs ninety-eight paragraphs in the *Patrologia Latina* text, Augustine takes up the issue of war in paragraphs seventy-four to seventy-six. He argues that what God commands is certainly not evil and asks what it is that is blamed in war? He answers that it is not that "human beings, who are going to die at some time, die so that others will be subdued and live in peace," but "the desire to do harm, cruelty in taking vengeance, a mind that is without peace and incapable of peace, fierceness in rebellion, the lust for domination, and anything else of that sort." He points out that "at the command of God or of some legitimate authority good men often undertake to wage wars" and again cites the preaching of John the Baptist and his guidance given to soldiers. For John knew that, when they killed as soldiers, "they were not murderers but ministers of the law, not avengers of injuries done to them but defenders of the public safety." Since the Manichees found fault with John the Baptist, Augustine points out that Christ himself taught that we should pay taxes and argues that "taxes are paid so that wages may be given to a soldier who is needed on account of wars." So too Jesus praised the faith of the centurion without commanding that he give up the army.[3]

Augustine saw that the causes and the authority under which war is waged are important. "The natural order which aims at the peace of mortals demands that the authority and decision to make war rest with the ruler, while soldiers have the duty of carrying out the commands of war for common peace and safety." Augustine argues that "it is not permissible to doubt that it is right to undertake a war which men undertake to wage under God's authority either to strike terror into, wear down, or subdue the pride of mortals." Although waging war under God's authority might seem to impose a limitation, Augustine appeals to *Romans* 13:1 and insists that "no one has any power unless it is given to him from above." Hence, he concludes that a just man fighting "under a godless human king...can correctly fight under his command so as to preserve the order of civil peace" — as long as "what is commanded is not against the commandment of God." The bishop of Hippo even explains that Christ's command "not to resist evil, but if anyone strikes you on the right check, offer him your left as well" (Mt 5:39) is not to be interpreted as a command against waging war, but has to do with a disposition of the heart, which was also present in the righteous men of the Old Testament.[4]

The whole thrust of the discussion of war is a defense of Moses and the other holy men of old who waged war under God's command and a rebuttal of the ignorance of the Manichees who ignorantly criticized the holy men of the Old Testament.

The symposia and discussions in the present volume face more complex and difficult issues, it would seem, than Augustine faced in his provincial city of Hippo. Augustine's position on war moved from a rather strict form of Christian pacifism in his early dialogue to a clear approval of war under legitimate authority for the right motives and carried out with certain limitations and in an acceptable manner in his later works. In the mature works he seems to regard the motives for waging war as most decisive, but certainly has come in the face of the barbarian invasions of Africa and other parts of the Roman empire to a realization that war may be a great evil, but is certainly necessary in certain cases. His stance toward war is hardly a full-blown theory, but it does reveal to us the mental development of a man who confronted the terrible reality of war and was ready to adapt his thinking to the demands of the current situation, as long as the action did not go against the commandments of God. He showed a good deal of flexibility in the face of changing circumstances. And were he able to be present at the symposia and discussions in the present volume, he would, I suspect, welcome the intelligent discussion of the issues and join right in, while scrambling to catch up on the complications of justifying a war in our present age with its weapons of mass destruction, with terrorist attacks upon civilian targets, and with all the current forms of the lust of domination. Augustine's confrontation with the evils of war in his mature years was not so much the application of a set of rules, such as some versions of the just-war theory present, but an exercise in practical wisdom in confrontation with the difficult and changing situation of the time. The authors of the articles in this volume clearly illustrate that the application of practical wisdom to the concrete situations of our contemporary wars in Iraq and Afghanistan is certainly as demanding and surely more challenging in many ways than it was in the era of Augustine of Hippo.

Notes

[1] Augustine, *De libero arbitrio* 1, 5, 12-13; PL 32: 1228.
[2] Augustine, *Epistola* 189, 4-6; PL 33: 855-856.
[3] Augustine, *Contra Faustum Manichaeum* 22, 74; PL 42: 447.
[4] Augustine, *Contra Faustum Manichaeum* 22, 75-76: PL 42: 448.

INTRODUCTION

Confessions, Contentions and the Lust for Power

Craig J. N. de Paulo, Patrick A. Messina
and Daniel P. Tompkins

Since the time of St. Augustine, the weightiest of thinkers in the Catholic tradition have pondered how Christian leaders should approach armed conflict. We use the term "Christian *leaders*" advisedly, since the Church's long establishment as a state religion, a century old in Augustine's day, brought with it particular obligations for state leadership, distinct from the obligations of the "food for powder" infantry recruited, for instance, by Shakespeare's Falstaff to march to the leaders' command.[1] Unlike Falstaff, the *Augustinian* leader has a conscience; and thus, a heavy concern for the "pitiful rascals" (another Shakespeare term) who serve or oppose him, for the vulnerable noncombatants behind the lines, and for the state that he or she is obliged to defend. Thus, Augustine stresses the authority of Moses in *Exodus* 32 while minimizing the role of the Levites. Leaders who, unlike Moses, cannot communicate directly with the Deity, carry the heavy burden of "prudential judgment."[2]

THE PROBLEM OF PRUDENTIAL JUDGMENT AND THE LUST FOR POWER

Indeed, it seems that anyone interested in entertaining the assumption that warfare can be, at least at times, justifiable, would find oneself struggling with the problem of prudential judgment since the just war principles themselves are called into action by a nation's leadership and his or her own decision making. Therefore, the strength of these venerable principles is ultimately put to the test by their reliance upon an individual moral determination. In this way, these moral universals are subject to an individual perception of justice since the respective ruler has the burden of finding certainty out of the ambiguity of what is more often than not a situation of fear and what is classically called the "lust for power."[3]

Further, it seems that the significance of prudential judgment in the just war tradition permits simple assumptions about human nature: that there are good rulers and bad rulers, and that the good rulers must be using prudential judgment well in which case, we can conclude that their wars are morally justifiable. Whereas, we also seem to assume that bad rulers cannot possibly be using prudential judgment well; and thus, cannot justify war. While the realms of good and evil may be simply divided, this logic seems overly simplistic and problematic. The ruler, or leader, who may think that he or she has a handle on the complex circumstances that lead to the decision of waging war must contend with the often conflicting, personal motivations that push judgment to rationalize rather than analyze. Our lust for power can influence the virtue of prudence to emphasize one's own shrewdness in making excuses to wage war instead of struggling with the moral consequence of proceeding with the choice of violence. What many just war theorists today seem to ignore about the theory is actually quite essential, as we will see in the sources—that is to say, that at least within the Christian tradition, war is always the result of the failure of peace and the consequence of sin. Furthermore, the theory must also take into consideration the fundamental (theological) assumption that man is good, but corrupt; and thus, the virtue of prudence is also vulnerable to human fallenness. Prudence must be reflective, which is to say, that it must realize its own sinful inclination, as a result of original sin, leading to its profound limitation so often overlooked by contemporary theorists. Therefore, if prudential judgment is to be of any value it must be honest about its potential for error rather than risk growing over confident about its surety. In fact, in the Christian (Augustinian) tradition, the prudent leader must even somehow include the Gospel paradox of "loving the enemy" in the very decision to wage war and in the subsequent conduct of war. Historically speaking, on the one hand, the Christian tradition wholeheartedly affirms that war is the result of sin; yet, on the other hand, at least in terms of Western Christianity, war has always been viewed as necessary at times to battle the enemy whether spiritual or otherwise.[4]

THE FIRST SYMPOSIUM ON JUST WAR THEORY AND THE WARS IN AFGHANISTAN AND IRAQ

The Call to Arms and the Current Controversy of War

On March 19, 2003, then President George W. Bush announced the United States led coalition attack on the sovereign nation of Iraq. The immediate strategic goal was conveyed to all as simple and straight forward: to oust by forcible means the troublesome regime of Sadaam Hussein.[5] The broader long-term goal, however, seems to have been more complex, arduous and controversial: to supplant an unfriendly, threatening presence in a vital economic and strategic region with a more friendly, Western-leaning government that could provide a springboard effect for the further democratization of the entire Middle East region.[6] This grand and seemingly noble strategic plan has from the start sparked controversy regarding the authentic, moral rationale for waging war against a sovereign Iraq, as well as understanding the role of the previous—albeit ongoing—Afghan War in bringing about this larger geo-political vision of a more democratic Middle East. Even though the Iraq War seemed then as now to dominate the landscape of moral controversy, the Afghan conflict was never really devoid of its own moral critics, nor has it suffered any dearth of depiction as the Iraq War's preceding strategic companion in the over-arching war against terror.

In support of this "noble strategy" there have been offered several ancillary arguments that have collectively become a *sine qua non* for establishing the moral justification of the Iraq war; for example, the destruction of Saddam Hussein's Weapons of Mass Destruction (WMD) program (a claimed threat to the security and stability of the region), the elimination of an important sponsor of the terrorist cause, an end to a regime guilty of committing genocide against its Kurdish population, the liberation of the entire Iraqi population from a megalomaniacal, malevolent dictator, just to name a few. It is the first of these "ancillary" justifications that, in fact, emerged as the most compelling and subsequently dubious reason for taking "decisive" military action in bringing a final end to Saddam Hussein's rule. However, the growing font of contravening facts as to the presence of WMDs in Saddam Hussein's Iraq has brought many Americans to the distasteful conclusion that no matter how well intended the Bush administration may have been in its decision to go to war with Iraq, its choice to employ what one may now call a factually deficient *terreur politique* has cast serious doubts on the entire complex of justifications for the conflict. The result has been a vast moral reconsideration of the decision to embark upon what many believe to be the first definitive example of preemptive war initiated by the United States.[7] While this moral re-consideration has come from diverse political and religious sources both within the United States and abroad, our intention is not so much to survey all these sources, or even to offer another moral solution as such; but to further contribute to the ethical discussion of these issues in an attempt to discover whatever moral legitimacy of the wars in Afghanistan and Iraq may or may not exist.

Directly following the military incursions into Afghanistan and Iraq, Professor Craig de Paulo was responsible for organizing two symposia intended to bring together prominent American voices taken from academia, the clergy, the military and the diplomatic corps that would engage the current crisis of war with intellectual honesty and debate. The symposia were inspired by the words of Bishop Wilton Gregory, then President of the United States Conference of Catholic Bishops, who wrote, "We urge Catholics, especially lay men and women who are called to be 'leaven' in society, to continue to think deeply about the choices we face, to review carefully the teaching of our Church and to speak out strongly in accord with their conscience."[8]

The first of these two events occurred on December 6, 2004 at the Union League of Philadelphia. It was a formal symposium on the question of Catholic just war theory and its application to the wars in Afghanistan and Iraq, which was attended by over four hundred and fifty people, including the media. The symposium panel consisted of a diverse and highly prominent group of scholars and foreign policy makers, including Professor John D. Caputo, a very distinguished philosopher and scholar, Avery Cardinal Dulles, S.J., a renowned scholar and theologian, Dr. Joseph H. Hagan, President Emeritus of Assumption College, Colonel Jack Jacobs, a retired U.S. Army officer, Medal of Honor recipient and MSNBC Military analyst, Mr. George J. Marlin, a conservative political commentator and former Executive Director of the Port Authority of New York and New Jersey, Ambassador Thomas Melady, former U. S. Ambassador to the Holy See, and Archbishop Edwin F. O'Brien, then Archbishop of the U.S. Military Archdiocese and Head of Catholic Military Chaplains. In his capacity as moderator, Professor de Paulo, asked pointed questions to this panel on everything from the moral validity of the wars, to the role of the Catholic Church in providing a moral compass for citizens as well as military personnel.

The second event which took place on March 28, 2006 also at the Union League of Philadelphia was intended to pursue some of the issues that were raised in the previous discussion in a more philosophically precise manner with expert theologians and philosophers. In this 2006 symposium, the panelists considered the just war theory principles themselves as to their own moral or conceptual sufficiency as well as a more detailed examination of the role of the papacy in guiding Catholic soldiers with respect to the moral acceptance or rejection of the wars in question. The reasoning behind the decision to have two symposia was intended to

encourage a more balanced discussion of these wars, the principles of just war theory and the role of conscience.

Panelists from both events were asked to consider the moral
legitimacy of the wars in accordance with what have become the
six benchmark principles of what is often referred to as *"ad bellum"* just war doctrine: 1) legitimate authority, 2) just cause, 3)
right intention, 4) proportionality, 5) likelihood of success and 6)
last resort.[9] While at least three of these principles are ancient in
origin and can be easily traced back to their Greek, Roman and
Christian sources, the entire list of principles represent more than
two millennia of the developing tradition.[10]

CONFESSIONS, CONTENTIONS AND CONFUSION

One of the first to speak at the 2004 gathering was conservative political commentator, George J. Marlin, who stressed the
high level of danger sites like the World Trade Center faced daily
in his former capacity as Executive Director of the Port Authority
of New York and New Jersey. He argued that preemption against
future terrorism necessitated American action in Iraq, and eloquently described the human suffering of New York neighbor-
hoods after the attacks of September 11, 2001: "We have," he said,
"an obligation by judgment of moral obligations to use every preventive measure we can take hold of to make sure that does not
happen again." As an advocate for preemptive war, Marlin supports the position that the current dangers of terrorism require a
new perspective concerning the moral evaluation of a nation's
right to go to war. Like other conservative thinkers, Marlin favors
a strong executive, assuming the leader's right to discern the necessity of war without foreign interference. Thus, Marlin seems to
represent that position largely promoted by conservative voices in
the United States, particularly among the Catholic intelligentsia,
that the ultimate decision for warfare depends upon the prudential judgment of the leader and that religious influences ought to
defer to secular authority.[11] Needless to say, this position reflects
the constitutional separation of Church and State without any intended disrespect toward the pope or the Church. By contrast,
however, the so-called "liberal" Catholics would argue that the

above conservative position is inherently contradictory. That is to say, that Catholic conservatives cannot hold the position that the pope's moral authority ought to extend to every political decision involving life, except that of waging war.

The question of prudential judgment and its role in relation to just war principles was taken up again by the eminent theologian, Cardinal Avery Dulles, S.J., who summarized the unchanging "principles" of just war, then argued that the "practices" of just warfare must be adapted to fit the circumstances: "The rules of just war theory, as contrasted with the principles, change according to the evolving methods of warfare," such as nuclear war and borderless terrorism. Sagely warning us that "one should not expect too much from the principles," Cardinal Dulles underscored the need of "prudent judgment," without which "the principles could be abused to support an unjust war or to forbid a just one." Again, he states, "That part of the world where terrorism is being bred" was a matter of particular concern, requiring allied action: Saddam Hussein, he said, brought the world "to the point of last resort."

Turning to the vexed question of whether a papal opinion on a coming war should be authoritative, Cardinal Dulles distinguished between doctrinal and "conventional" matters and noted that Pope John Paul II "never said that the war is unjust or would trouble the conscience of the people engaged in the military." Taking up the "principles" of just war, he stated that the war in Iraq "certainly has a right intention and just cause and could be legitimate authority to wage humanitarian intervention."

Cardinal Dulles concluded unequivocally that, based upon the principles of just war theory, in his estimation, the war in Iraq was just. He also gave good insight to the problem of prudential judgment by acknowledging the disparity between the principles and their application. However, Dulles' Thomistic position relies heavily upon the certitude of the virtue of prudence to manage this problem and attempt to resolve this disparity. This position further assumes the soundness of the leader's prudential judgment simply by virtue of his or her office; and thereby, harkening an ancient sense of anointed power, which might be easily criticized by contemporary theorists wanting to protect democratic processes.

Ambassador Thomas Melady, who was heavily involved in negotiations prior to the First Gulf War, spoke with intimate knowledge of the diplomatic background. He dismissed any suggestions of "passivity" when confronting an enemy. For Melady, as for other conservative speakers, the prudential authority of the civilian leadership was again central. Turning to particulars, Ambassador Melady reviewed the discussions over the First and Second Gulf War, and added that John Paul II has never said that the Second Gulf war "is immoral," and that the pope had supported military intervention in Somalia and Liberia. "The motive [for Gulf War II] was right, and now that we did that," he argued, "I'm clear that we should win the war with dignity and honor and proceed to other matters."

Archbishop Edwin O' Brien also emphasized prudential judgment, although recognizing its elusiveness. The Archbishop first insisted that he was not a specialist on international relations, and he cited the finding of the American Bishops "that there were sufficient arguments on either side to allow a prudent person to come down [on] either side [as to] whether the war is justified or not." He continued by saying that the Bush administration, convinced that "there were stockpiles of weapons in Iraq...[acted] in good faith." Again, for Archbishop O'Brien, as with many others on the panel, the "prudence" of the civilian authority was essential. Speaking as "one in the military," he said, "we must have faith in our government." Again like others, he attempted to categorize the pope's position with care, mentioning that the Vatican diplomat, then Cardinal Pio Laghi "said the pope has not proposed the position as the doctrine of the Church, but as the appeal of conscience illuminated by the faith." Asked whether the war in Iraq was unjust, he said, "It's not clear, I don't think it's actually clear enough to make an undisputed one-sided decision."

What is interesting to note in Archbishop O' Brien's position is his statement about having "faith in our government." Although the Archbishop was certainly in a difficult position, as both a high-ranking member of the clergy and then the Catholic Head of Chaplains for the U.S. military, his exhortation was somewhat unexpected, despite its ancient and apostolic roots, since it assumes the intrinsic goodness of the government and the goodness of secular leadership. It further assumes a more intimate relationship between Church and State that seems more ancient than modern; and, once again, a position that could be readily criticized today for not heeding the overwhelming opposition of the people.

In contradistinction to Archbishop O'Brien's point of view, the renowned philosopher, Professor John D. Caputo, returned the discussion back to several earlier questions from a different point of view and argued for a position of skepticism with regard to our relationship with the government. "Every assumption that we made [in moving preemptively] has proved to be wrong," he said, "and military preemption, like capital punishment, permits no coming back." "The consequences," he said, are "costing lives, costing money, it's costing the prestige of the United States as a moral leader." Unlike many of the other panelists present, Professor Caputo portrayed the "intent" of the United States government in Iraq as "shifting," offering new justifications as old ones fail, and stated that the religious language of the administration "implicitly... appeal [s] to the Christian Right."

Perhaps what was most startling about this first symposium was the confusion over the Church's position on whether these wars were to be considered just or unjust. There was also, and perhaps rightfully so, a great deal of confusion over Pope John Paul II's position on these wars. And, there are number of questions that remain and continue to plague us. For instance, What is the meaning of the pontiff's position when it is given diplomatically in the person of one of his envoys or by way of an Apostolic Nuncio? Surely, these diplomatic positions reflect the mind of the pontiff as a head of state, but what influence should they have on our nation's leadership and especially on Catholic citizens? There is also a great deal of confusion over the status of the official position of the United States Conference of Catholic Bishops, and their respective statements on the wars, which did not seem to play a significant role in the positions taken by most of our panelists in the first symposium, including the clergy. In fact, the pontiff's position on these wars had a great deal of exposure in the press and was clearly established, yet it was unclear to many of our distinguished panelists, who may have been challenging the right of the pontiff to interfere with the business of the state.[12] There was also the question as to how we ought to categorize the pontiff's remarks since he was not necessarily speaking from a position of the Magisterium; and therefore, most Catholic "conservatives" might conclude that the pontiff's position is simply an opinion and not binding upon Catholics. While this would be true, what is the significance of the statements made by the pontiff, his diplomats and his College of Bishops for the faithful? More importantly, what effect might these statements have on conscience? And, even more radically, what are the moral consequences for Christians, and especially Catholics, if they are serving in an unjust war? Thus, in order to set the record straight, let us consider some of the several statements made by the Church concerning the war in Iraq.

SOME CLARIFICATION ON THE ECCLESIASTICAL STATEMENTS

On November 13, 2002, the United States Conference of Catholic Bishops published a "Statement on Iraq," stating that:

> Two months ago, Bishop Wilton Gregory, President of the United States Conference of Catholic Bishops, wrote President George Bush to welcome efforts to focus the world's attention on Iraq's refusal to comply with several United Nations resolutions over the past eleven years, and its pursuit of weapons of mass destruction. This letter, which was authorized by the U.S. Bishop's Administrative Committee, raised serious questions about the moral legitimacy of any preemptive, unilateral use of military force to overthrow the government of Iraq. As a body, we make our own the questions and concerns raised in Bishop Gregory's letter, taking into account developments since then, especially the unanimous action of the U. N. Security Council on November 8th.[13]

This USCCB statement goes on to say boldly that "with the Holy See and bishops from the Middle East and around the world, we fear that resort to war, under present circumstances and in light of current public information, would not meet the strict conditions in Catholic teaching for overriding the strong presumption against the use of military force."[14] Needless to say, this statement assumes the clarity of the position of the Holy See and the College of

Bishops from around the world, something that was disputed by several of the panelists in the first symposium.

On February 19, 2003, Bishop Celestino Migliore, the Apostolic Nuncio to the United Nations in New York, addressed the U. N. Chamber of the Security Council on the Iraqi issue, stating, "The Holy See is convinced that in the efforts to draw strength from the wealth of peaceful tools provided by the international law, to resort to force would not be a just one."[15] Again, here is another clear and unequivocal statement concerning that the Holy See considered the war in Iraq unjust. Bishop Migliore goes on to say, "The Holy See encourages the parties concerned to keep the dialogue open that could bring about solutions in preventing a possible war and urges the international community to assume its responsibility in dealing with any failings by Iraq."[16] Setting the moral standard, the Holy See remained committed to conversation rather conflict.

Again, on February 26, 2003, the United States Conference of Catholic Bishops issued another "Statement on Iraq" authored by then USCCB President, Bishop Wilton D. Gregory:

> We join with Pope John Paul in the conviction that war is not "inevitable" and that "war is always a defeat for humanity." This is not a matter of ends, but means. Our bishop's conference continues to question the moral legitimacy of any preemptive, unilateral use of military force to overthrow the government of Iraq. To permit preemptive or preventive use of military force to overthrow threatening or hostile regimes would create deeply troubling moral and legal precedents. Based on the facts that are known, it is difficult to justify resort to war against Iraq, lacking clear and adequate evidence of an imminent attack of a grave nature or Iraq's involvement in the terrorist attacks of September 11. With the Holy See and many religious leaders throughout the world, we believe that resort to war would not meet the strict conditions in Catholic teaching for the use of military force.[17]

Although the USCCB statements are often ignored (and sometimes even ridiculed) by neoconservatives today, the Bishops eloquently argue their case based upon sound reasoning and tradition, stating that a preemptive military strike would clearly be inconsistent with traditional Catholic teaching. Citing the authority of Pope John Paul II and the Church's magisterium, the

U.S. Bishops concluded that war in Iraq would be unjust. Once again, the question arises, how can a so-called "conservative" Catholic disregard so many authoritative exhortations from the hierarchy, including the pope and the national episcopal conference? Bishop Gregory continues by stating, "We hope and pray that leaders in Iraq, the United Nations and in our own land will hear and heed the persistent pleas of Pope John Paul II to take concrete steps to avoid war and build peace based on respect for international law and for all human life."[18]

Although it would not be considered as an official document of the Church, it is worthy to mention that the Social Justice Secretariat of the Society of Jesus in Rome, sent a letter on February 7, 2003 to each of the Jesuit Provinces around the world, concisely outlining their opposition to a war with Iraq. In this letter signed by Fr. Fernando Franco, S.J., the Jesuit Order stated its case in five points:

> 1) The "doctrine" of preemptive war is neither in accordance with UN doctrine and law, nor morally defensible. The application of this doctrine would open the door to an infinite war, a "war without end." 2) A war against Iraq would heighten tensions between Muslims and Christians in the Middle East and beyond. 3) A willingness to spend massive amounts of money on military action but not on development aid makes one ask "whether the true motives of war against Iraq have to do more with economic than security reasons." 4) The push for war is being made "unilaterally by the leaders of a few industrialized countries outside the control of the UN," and the United States and its allies seem to have disregarded the "obligation to build a broader consensus through legitimate democratic processes." 5) Experience has shown us that the poor are always the main victims of violence and war.[19]

In this statement, the Jesuits also raise the question of the hypocrisy of those who might argue for a just cause or right intention for the war in Iraq in their above sincere contention that the war was widely regarded as motivated more by economic concerns. Furthermore, the Jesuits are also concerned with the Iraqi people, and especially the poor, who as innocents, would greatly suffer from a war. Finally, the Jesuit position seems to support the Vatican position that such a terrible decision (*i.e.*, to go to war) should involve the larger international community including the United Nations.

On March 5, 2003, Pope John Paul II sent then Cardinal Pio Laghi as a papal envoy to meet with then President George W. Bush. Although the communication was secret, Cardinal Laghi issued a statement, saying, "The Holy See maintains that there are still peaceful avenues within the context of the vast patrimony of international law and institutions which exist for that purpose."[20] Nevertheless, it was widely speculated that the pope sent a special request to the president, asking him not to go to war on the grounds of its lack of justice. The cardinal concluded by saying that he told the president that on that day, Ash Wednesday, "Catholics around the world are following the Pope's request to pray and fast for peace this day."[21] Unfortunately, prayer and fasting did not prevent this war, but it powerfully demonstrates the seriousness of the Holy See in its determination to prevent this war.

Once again, Bishop Wilton Gregory, as USCCB President, issued yet another "Statement on the War with Iraq," on March 19, 2003, saying, "Our conference's moral concerns and questions, as well as the call of the Holy Father to find alternatives to war, are well known and reflect our prudential judgments about the application of traditional Catholic teaching on the use of force in this case...Echoing the Holy Father's admonition that war 'is always a defeat for humanity,' we have prayed and urged that peaceful means be pursued to disarm Iraq under UN auspices."[22] As the record shows, the Catholic Church through the diplomacy of the Holy See and the College of Bishops clearly stated their position that war is to be avoided as much as possible (and that a preemptive war can never be regarded as just, according to traditional Catholic principles); and that, the forlorn decision to go to war can only be pursued after all other (diplomatic) means have been exhausted. The Church also clearly supports the ideals and the mission of the United Nations and its vital role in resolving international conflicts.

The Second Symposium on Just War Theory, the 2003 War in Iraq and the Significance of the Papacy

Fifteen months later, again at the Union League, and again with Dr. Craig de Paulo as the Moderator, a different group of scholars, mostly philosophers and theologians, met with a more focused discussion. The first part of the session dealt specifically with the status of papal pronouncements about the Iraq War, and was handled by Professor Craig de Paulo, Professor Frederick Van Fleteren, Professor Brian Kane, Professor Joseph Margolis and Professor Daniel Tompkins, who commented during the first hour and played a larger role in the second hour, which focused on just war theology in general.

A large part of the first hour concerned "authority," specifically the capacity of various church officials to speak authoritatively about the Iraq War, but also, as Professor Margolis expressed it, the "deeper question about the possibilities of demonstrating the validity of moral...political positions." This elicited from Professor Van Fleteren the fascinating formulation that "just war theory has been a rational attempt to come to grips with what are essentially irrational situations."

The difficulty of invoking papal opinion to support or condemn particular wars was brought home by Professor Kane, who noted that John Paul II is the only Twentieth century pope who has "made definitive statements on the morality of any wars." The remainder of the first half of this session revolved around questions of authority and methodology, with Professor Margolis declaring that "the discussion of just war and...terrorism is in a shambles right now...None has a really promising way of relating systematically the analysis of terrorism to the analysis of war in terms of the just war traditions...And that means that the just war theory, if it is revived, has to be radically reformed in terms of this kind of slippage."

In the second half of this session, all participants discussed the various applications of just war theory, under the prompting of Professor Patrick Messina. One high point came with Professor Kane's reference to the papal Encyclical *Evangelium Vitae* (1995), on the value of human life: "The real purpose of civil law is to guarantee an order in social existence in true justice so that all may lead a quiet and peaceful life." Thus, Professor Kane concluded, "Legitimate authority is always related to the end of community." The homology or congruence between authority in peace and authority in war, nicely captured in two successive chapters of *The City of God*, is not only elegant in itself, but points to the shared *telos* of the judge's and the general's *praxis*: protect the community – and the community has evolved, since the Peace of Westphalia (1648), into the sovereign state. Under just war theory, state sovereignty acquires almost sacred status, a topic we shall continue with later.

THE FUTURE OF THE WORLD ORDER AND THE IMPLICATIONS OF THE WAR IN IRAQ ON INTERNATIONAL LAW

This essay by Professor Dieter Blumenwitz, which appears in chapter four, is a serious meditation on the origin of just war theory in ancient traditions governing the law of nations and the prospects for the future, with an emphasis on the above concept, which we will return to shortly: the sovereign equality of each nation-state. Relying primarily on Hugo Grotius' *De Jure Belli ac Pacis (On the Law of War and Peace)* (1625), Blumenwitz is quick to point out the danger inherent in just war theory: inherently malleable and subjective in application, it allows "each nation" to judge the justice of an intended war, using "criteria so vague that it is possible for every belligerent nation to project its war as just." Blumenwitz traces the key developments covering the law of war from 1625 to the present: Grotius' prohibition against wars "to prevent the growth of a power which…could become dangerous"; The Hague Convention on Land Warfare (1899); the Charter of the United Nations (1945) which answered the *Quis judicabit?* question by "disenfranchis[ing] member nations from taking unilateral action"; the UN General Assembly's development in 1974 of a "comprehensive definition of aggression" that significantly extended to "humanitarian intervention and preventive war, with its philanthropic and euphemistic phrases."

All of this is now at risk, according to Blumenwitz, as a single world *hegemon* seizes control of decision-making. The (1992) "Defense Planning Guidance" of the United States urged both solo and preventative warfare, without recourse to the Security Council. He foresees "chaos in international relationships...if each nation unilaterally could decide on possible threat scenarios and on military measures which should be applied preventatively." Contemplating this danger, Blumenwitz puts his faith not in other great powers or in international organizations, but in "American civil society, which is less imperial and martial in its orientation than the neo-conservative strategists of the Bush administration and which has not yet lost its normative authority."

"NO SUBSTITUTE FOR THE FACTS"[23]

Any political leader contemplating "just warfare" carries a heavy burden. The principles of just war require an effort not only at purity of heart, but at accurate assessment of the situation before him or her: evidence and facts are required to judge the justice of the cause, to avoid endangering civilian populations, to consider alternative courses of action before this "last resort," to weigh the likely "prospects of success," and to assure that one will not cause "evils and disorders graver than the evil to be eliminated."

Terms like "facts" and "evidence" were used approximately twenty times during the first symposium. Readers in the future may find themselves unpacking the evidence all over again. As they do so, it will be important to remember that wars have a long "tail": a battle may result in few civilian deaths, for instance, but may damage water supplies and medical care, may leave a string of wounded or starving survivors, and may have catastrophic effects on civil order. Khruschev's famous warning, "The survivors will envy the dead," applies to many "conventional" conflicts as well as the nuclear war he had in mind.

Was the danger to Iraq's civilian population considered with true care? The point of the question is not simply, are Iraqis now suffering, but rather, was the possibility of their suffering weighed with the requisite care before the war began on March 20, 2003?

Were adequate plans being made to handle water, oil, and electricity, to manage civic unrest, and to provide medical care? Was the American argument for "weapons of mass destruction" conclusive? Was the international consensus behind the U.S. as firm, as many claimed? Can we say that we gave serious thought to the question of whether invasion would create "evils and disorders graver than the evil to be eliminated?"

Similarly, Americans will now be asking whether alternative courses of action were considered with care, and whether the invasion really was a "last resort"? They will note that the United Nations Monitoring, Verification and Inspection Commission continued investigating the situation in Iraq until March 18, 2003, two days before the invasion, and reported finding no evidence of weapons of mass destruction. Why did the American leadership not pay more attention to the pre-invasion indications that our informants were unreliable? One very serious "last resort" question, in the light of the ongoing inspections, was why the invasion had to begin precisely at the time it did?

Finally, Americans will ask whether the "prospects of success" were really as strong as advertised in 2003, and whether more attention should have been given to the prospects for a less than successful military adventure? All of the claims listed above were disputed in some detail in the press before the invasion.

With all of this in mind, the power of the *Catechism of the Catholic Church* stems in part from the seamlessness of its moral message. Starting with the simple four words of the Fifth Commandment: "Thou shall not kill," it builds a crescendo of argument that culminates in the lessons about war, ending with the admonition to "vanquish sin by coming together in charity." That moral lesson includes, "The strict conditions for *legitimate defense by military force*" (2309). In such a context, getting one's facts right and presenting them honestly becomes a religious obligation. History will tell us whether this was done before March 20, 2003.[24]

SOVEREIGNTY AND WARS OF CHOICE: AN AUGUSTINIAN *CAVEAT PRAEEMPTOR*

Augustine's *City of God* makes clear both that the earthly city is woefully imperfect and yet necessary.[25] It is the framework within which the leader impelled by the "obligation to care," *propter necessitatem caritatis,* takes up his burden.[26] Both Augustine and the *Catechism* of Pope John Paul II accept the role of the state.

And the state is consequential indeed. *Caritas*, as Augustine and the just war tradition envision it, would be meaningless without the borders or frontiers that define the sovereign state, and the notion of sovereignty became progressively more influential until it was given primacy in the Peace of Westphalia in 1648.

The challenge that arises for conscientious thinkers like Blumenwitz is that without a normative structure of international relations, powerful states will use their power to annul the statehood of the less powerful. The current state of Iraq is one example: from a state that held a more or less stable place in a dangerous part of the world, it has been reduced to what may become a "failed state," without a marginally functioning army or government and threatened with division into smaller sub-states, each of which will encounter tensions of its own.[27] Nevertheless, Iraq is evidently less chaotic today than it was only a few years ago, but problems remain. We cannot tell what will happen if Iraq is broken into pieces, or left as a "failed state" after an American departure. Certainly, one result of the American intervention has been the deaths of massive numbers of Iraqis, a second has been to encourage separatism in Kurdistan, and a third, to strengthen Iranian power in the region. Whether American interests have been served remains unclear. As Augustine might have said, *caveat praeemptor.*

This is not to say that Saddam Hussein in any way deserved to stay in power. But contemplation of the results of the invasion is a sobering reminder of the need for care in invading other states: we trifle with sovereignty at our peril.

AN AUGUSTINIAN WARNING: JUSTICE AND AMBIGUITY

Augustine constantly warns the reader that just wars might obscure into unjust wars. The just empire seeking to impose itself on its neighbors, to violate their sovereignty, may transmute into something less than just: *"inferre autem bella finitimis et in cetera inde procedere ac populos sibi non molestos sola regni cupiditate conterere et subdere, quid aliud quam grande latrocinium nominandum est?"*[28]

Although the conversion of Constantine brought the possibility of justice for the late Roman Empire, it did not assure it; and it is characteristic of Augustine to hedge the achievements of the earthly city with interrogatives, as in the passage just quoted. One paradox for just war theory is that justice must lie on one side only. And here a danger lies, since Augustine gives the impression that war does not occur, or should not occur, between two equally justified parties. Despite Augustine's insistence that the ruler must adhere to certain rules, he uses words like *"iniquitas"* (iniquity) and *"malum"* (evil) so often to refer to opponents that it is easy to understand how his followers might convince themselves of the rectitude of their own position and the wrongness of their opponents'. This may be especially likely since the judge and the ruler are so congruent, both foes of *malum*. The word "evildoer" has long roots and the *"libido dominandi"* can easily be applied to a ruler like Saddam Hussein, but we must always be aware of our own liability to *regni cupiditas*.

AUGUSTINIAN LEADERSHIP AND THE BURDEN OF CONSCIENCE

It is difficult to exaggerate how worthwhile the discussions of this book have been, not only for students of philosophy and theology, but for anyone interested in the possibility of standards that might govern international relations. Intellectually independent, at times unforgettably lucid, the contributions and the ensemble will retain their value in the coming decades. Indeed, the subject is too important and too terrible to reduce to the standards of "debate." Augustine is a serious guide in this – a Virgil in this journey to our Dante – because we can see his own decades-long intellectual journey in his work: "*quisquis autem uel patitur ea sine animi dolore uel cogitat, multo utique miserius ideo se putat beatum, quia et humanum perdidit sensum.*"[29]

As we have seen, the discussions in this book illustrate a huge dependence upon the prudential judgment of the leader in dealing with the "evil-doers." And, prudence, as Augustine wisely observed, is an elusive virtue. He writes, "*Quid illa uirtus, quae prudentia dicitur, nonne tota uigilantia sua bona discernit a malis, ut in illis appetendis istisque uitandis nullus error obrepat, ac per hoc et ipsa nos in malis uel mala in nobis esse testatur?*"[30] "*Nullus error:*" This is an arduous objective for a leader. The American Secretary of State Condoleezza Rice referred, in April 2006, to "thousands of tactical errors." In contrast, Augustine is full of praise for the leadership of the Roman Emperor, Constantine, but Constantine is a hard act to follow. In short, the progress in the world of Augustine's just warrior is one of constant *askesis*, and the danger of temptation is great. It is no wonder that scholars allude to the Bishop of Hippo's "mournful mood."[31]

Notes

[1] Shakespeare, *King Henry IV*, Part I, Act IV, Scene II.

[2] Augustine, *Contra Faustum*, XXII.74, *Bella gessit Moyses oboediens Deo recte iubenti* ("Moses waged wars in obedience to God who ordered him"); Michael Walzer, "Exodus 32 and the Theory of a Holy War: The History of a Citation," *Harvard Theological Review* 61 (1968) 1-14.

[3] St. Augustine termed this lust for power as "*libido dominandi.*" Cf. *De Civitate Dei* XIV.15; XIX.14.

[4] Byzantine (Greek), or Orthodox, Christianity does not have a theology of just war. Needless to say, it affirms the sinfulness of war and demands that Orthodox soldiers confess their sins and repent in order to return to communion in the Church even when a Christian emperor, in good conscience, has called for war.

[5] Cf. George W. Bush, "Address to the Nation from the Oval Office," (March 19, 2003): "Our nation enters this conflict reluctantly – yet, our purpose is sure. The people of the United States and our friends and allies will not live at the mercy of an outlaw regime…Now that conflict has come; the only way to limit its duration is to apply decisive force."

[6] The consensus on this position is so solid and widely published that citing an authoritative source seems tantamount to offering an extensive bibliography. However, Alexander J. Groth's article entitled, "Democratizing the Middle East:

A Conservative Perspective," *Journal of Libertarian Studies* vol. 19, no. 4, (Fall 2005), 3-17, appears to offer an adequate articulation of this consensus opinion only two years after the launch of the invasion.

[7] While this point may be argued to the contrary, the April 11, 2003 Congressional Research Service Report for Congress concluded the following in its Historical Overview: "The historical record indicates that the United States has never, to date, engaged in a preemptive military attack, as traditionally defined, against another nation." *CRS Report for Congress*, Richard F. Grimmett, Congressional Research Service, the Library of Congress (RS21311).

[8] Bishop Wilton Gregory, "Statement on Iraq" (February 26, 2003) www.usccb.org/sdwp/international/iraqstatement0203.htm.

[9] While some just war theorists include the distinct principle of comparative justice, the principle seems sufficiently represented within the more widely accepted just cause principle. Cf. Carl Ceulemans, "Just Cause," in *Moral Constraints on War*, ed. Bruno Coppieters and Nick Fotion (New York: Lexington Books, 2002), 36.

[10] Our brief history of just war theory in the West in chapter one will focus almost exclusively on the *ad bellum* principles.

[11] Such as George Weigel, Michael Novak, et. al.

[12] See Michael Griffin's article entitled, "New Pope Benedict XVI a Strong Critic of War," in *Houston Catholic Worker* Vol. XXV, no. 4 (special edition 2005) where he wrote, "This was perhaps what upset US neoconservatives most, that John Paul II and Cardinal Ratzinger did not show more deference to the state."

[13] "Statement on Iraq," published by the USCCB, Washington, DC (November 13, 2002), para. 2.

[14] *Ibid.*, para. 4.

[15] Cf. www.vatican.va/roman_curia/secretariat_state/2003/documents/rc_seg-st_20030219.

[16] *Ibid.*

[17] www.usccb.org/sdwp/international/iraqstatement0202.htm.

[18] *Ibid.*

[19] Cf. www.companysj.com/sjusa/030220.htm.

[20] Cf. www.usccb.org/comm/archives/2003/03-051.htm.

[21] *Ibid.*

[22] Cf. www.usccb.org/sdwp/peace/stm31903.htm.

[23] "There is no substitute for the facts" is quoted by Stanley Hauerwas and Paul J. Griffiths, "War, Peace and Jean Bethke Elshtain," *First Things* 136 (October 2003), 41.

[24] Another author who advertises his devotion to "empirical analysis" is George Weigel, *Witness to Hope: The Biography of Pope John Paul II* (New York: HarperCollins, 1999), 624. Weigel accuses the Vatican of failing to undertake a "rigorous empirical analysis" before opposing the first Gulf War. A page before, Weigel refers to the "failures in the endgame of the war, which were caused in part by...phobia about long-term U.S. involvement in reconstructing a post-

Saddam Iraq." The carnage still visible three years after the American "mission" was "accomplished" may reveal that President George H. W. Bush and General Colin Powell were prudent leaders in refusing to overthrow Saddam Hussein at the end of the first Gulf War. Weigel's cavalier treatment of harsh international realities is thrown into relief by his insistence that he, and not the Pope, was realistic and "empirical" in 1991.

[25] Augustine, *City of God* IXX.6.

[26] Augustine, *City of God* IXX.19.

[27] For instance, Kurdistan already has problems with both Turkey and Iran, not to mention a population of 750,000 restive Turkmen in Kirkuk.

[28] Augustine, *City of God* IV.6: "To impose wars on others...and to wear down and subdue peoples not harmful to oneself, with the single goal of rule, what can we call that but major theft?"

[29] Augustine, *The City of God against the Pagans*, ed. and trans. by R. W. Dyson (Cambridge: Cambridge University Press, 1998) XIX.7: "And if anyone either endures them or thinks of them without anguish of soul, his condition is still more miserable; for he thinks himself happy only because he has lost all human feeling."

[30] Augustine, *City of God* IXX.4: "What shall I say of that virtue, which is called prudence? Is not all its vigilance spent in the discernment of good from evil things, so that no mistake may be admitted about what we should desire and what avoid? And thus it is itself a proof that we are in the midst of evils, or that evils are in us."

[31] Roland H. Bainton, *Christian Attitudes Toward War and Peace* (New York: Abington Press, 1960), 98-9.

CHAPTER ONE

The Influence of Augustine on the Development of Just War Theory

Patrick A. Messina and Craig J. N. de Paulo
Gwynedd Mercy College

B efore we begin to address the pervasive influence of the great Augustine of Hippo on what will become the just war tradition in Western Christendom, let us first say a few words on the ancient Greeks and Romans whose early speculation raised the question of justifiable violence in their war-driven civilizations. Now, while the question of a just war first appears in pagan Greco-Roman thought, its achievements are limited by its historical circumstances and, in particular, its cultural acceptance and economic dependence upon slavery. Moreover, the ancient lust for glory, dominion and empire is precisely what reveals the most formidable shortcoming in the Greek and Roman philosophers and their societies. For these reasons, the ancient pre-Christian ideas on the topic are simply not enduring since they lack a fundamental appreciation for the dignity of human life and the moral imperative of human rights. Thus, it is St. Augustine who is rightfully considered the founder of just war theory because he was the first to articulate the perennial criteria within the framework of the Christian *ethos* of love and equality as human beings made in the image and likeness of the Creator.

EARLY GRECO-ROMAN SPECULATION

While it seems unlikely that Aristotle was the first thinker to contemplate the notion of just war in the West,[1] he was the earliest thinker to consider it systematically, situating it within the greater scheme of political science.[2] In his *Politics*, Aristotle not only recognizes the necessity of war and its ultimate aim of peace and leisure,[3] but he also formulates what appears to be the tradition's first draft of just cause criteria: war is justified in order to 1) avoid enslavement; 2) establish empire for the good of the governed; and 3) enslave those disposed by nature to be enslaved.[4] Of these three principles, the only one that has retained any semblance of Contemporary relevance is the first. The latter two, rooted as they are in the Ancient assumption of slavery, have today been reduced to what one might call an anathematized anachronism. The problems of his well-known moral acceptance of slavery notwithstanding, Aristotle's insistence on a state's right to ward off enemy dominion and remain free and autonomous is fundamental to much of just war theory.

Later, Roman philosophers would have to consider the right reasons to wage war according to their own manifold political circumstances, and the most prestigious name would have to be Cicero. Cicero's contribution was significant with regard to both *in bello* and *ad bellum* principles. In his work, *De Officis*, he offers a more emphatic and somewhat comprehensive imperative of just cause for any military engagement. Like Aristotle before him, Cicero sees peace and justice as the proper ends.[5] In addition to this, he seems to conceive the just cause principle as the endeavor to exact retribution and punishment (*ulciscendi et puniendi*)[6] on the enemy for injuries incurred (*a quibus iniuriam acceperis*),[7] preceded of course by a prior declaration of intent.[8] Again, like Aristotle, Cicero also considered the quest for empire justifiable (*bella quibus imperii proposita gloria est*) so long as it secured a *pax Romana* for the greater and common good.[9] In fact, private war could never be justified, since the state's moral authority to wage war stood in tandem with its responsibility to provide the common weal.[10]

One might further interpret from Cicero's ruminations in *De Officiis* the seeds of both the proportionality and the last resort principles.[11] Regarding proportionality, one need only refer again to the final lines of Book I, 33 where Cicero speaks of maintaining a certain limit or "measure" (*modus*) in administering just retribution on an enemy (*est enim ulciscendi et puniendi modus*).[12] Although he never actually elaborates on the specifics of this measure, the notion of proportion as an avoidance of extremes is clearly mentioned in association with the very essence of just cause (*ulciscendi et puniendi*).[13] As for the last resort principle, Cicero suggests that violence against an enemy should only be waged when a rational solution to conflict has been deemed impossible; thus he eloquently states:

> For since there are two ways of settling a dispute: first by discussion; second by physical force; and since the former is characteristic of man, the latter the brute, we must resort to force only in case we may not avail ourselves of discussion.[14]

Again, the fullness of the modern principle may by lacking, but the seminal idea is unmistakably present in the preference of reasonable discourse to armed violence.

Finally, when discussing the topic of war, there are times when Cicero's rhetorical tone inclines toward the presumption against war. On the one hand, when he speaks of courage and the kind of activity to which it properly belongs, he places the virtue in the soul and spirit of the one who prevents armed conflict rather than in the one who courts it.[15] And in perfect classical character, Cicero then extends the condition of the soul to the organs of government when he firmly declares that achievements of civic effort far exceed in virtue the achievements of military effort.[16] In conjunction, these two sentiments give the decisive, summary impression that Cicero finds peaceful engagement between states far more civilized and virtuous than the state of war.[17]

AUGUSTINE, FOUNDER OF CHRISTIAN JUST WAR THEORY

As the bridge not only between the late Roman Empire and the Middle Ages, but also between Greco-Roman thought and Christianity, St. Augustine is the most significant figure in the development of just war thought. In fact, Augustine is almost unanimously considered by scholars to be the father of the theory in the West.[18] That is not to say that he was the first or only thinker (Latin or Greek) to weigh in on the issue of just war during the patristic age, but he was surely responsible for the fundamental rubric of just war principles that continue to be used today. Like Cicero, Augustine did not give a systematic treatment of just cause, but it was Augustine's ingenious idea to shift the moral focus for the justification of war on the supernatural phenomenon of Christian love, trumping as it were, the classical yet natural virtue of justice.[19] In some sense, in keeping with this shifting focus, one might call Augustine's vision of just war a war of loves and that even war must be governed by love as much as possible. For Augustine, war could only be justified if the condition of the warrior's soul were somehow inspired by the love of God and neighbor.[20] Within this notion, Augustine retains Cicero's basic definition of just cause as the redress of and punishment for incurred injuries (*ulciscendi et puniendi*),[21] yet he masterfully introduces the importance of interior motives thereby establishing the principle of right intention. According to this principle, the one who wages war must administer vengeance (*viz.*, wage war) out of a desire for the Good, which many scholars conclude, may also involve punitive correction and even rehabilitation of the transgressor in much the same way as leaders admonish their own citizens, or parents, their children.[22] This Augustinian kind of solicitude for the moral integrity of the transgressor, it is speculated, guarantees a loving disposition in the leader who chooses war as a means of redressing injustices imposed upon those over whom he is commissioned to protect.[23]

There is little doubt about the moral stringency of this principle that requires not only the aforementioned solicitude but an avoidance of all types of wrong desire that may corrupt the intentions of one who wages war. Thus, the famous passage from Augustine's *Contra Faustum* outlines the conditions for a rightly ordered intention in the context of his just war theory:

> The desire for harming, the cruelty of revenge, the restless and implacable mind, the savageness of revolting, the lust for dominating, and similar things — these are what are justly blamed in wars.[24]

Hence, it is not enough for the leader waging war to have a just cause (even one as noble as protecting the innocent), he must also love the belligerent with whom he is about to engage in violent conflict.[25] While this mystical prescription of love is admirable, to say the least, most realists might easily argue, impossible. Augustine's response: indeed, but ideally speaking, the Christian leader must live a mystical and selfless life of love as God's anointed.

Furthermore, among the insidious desires that Augustine details above, the lust for domination (*libido dominandi*) may best underscore the paradoxical need for love (*caritas*) in the act of waging just war and further demonstrate how Augustine's own *idealism* with regard to *justum bellum* derives ultimately from his Christian anthropology and eschatology.[26] For Augustine, both the individual human soul and the political community as a whole are beset by inordinate desire (*libido, cupiditas, concupiscentia*).[27] This sinful condition derives from original sin, which, among other faults, produces a moral condition of weakness in the human being, genealogically connected to Adam and Eve's fall from grace. This weakness inclines the human will to desire its own, worldly satisfaction to the neglect of true fulfillment in God. However, as Augustine notes, God has granted His love (*caritas*) as a correction, infusing by grace what the corrupted will needs to desire and to choose what is morally right and genuinely good.[28] In effect, the human will is thus constituted by two contrary, commingling loves that bring conflict and confusion in desiring and choosing particular goods.[29] Due to the natural correspondence between the individual and the state,[30] the citizens and the body politic suffer from a fundamental conflict that, from desire to decision, often results in acts of violence and strife.[31] This projection of the soul's conflict onto the general conditions of the state inspired

Augustine to invoke Jerusalem and Babylon in order to meta-phorically explain the precarious state of the Christian in the world. Augustine's two cities have spiritual, political and cosmic dimensions: Jerusalem representing the kingdom of God on earth and in heaven (*caritas*) and Babylon representing the kingdom of man (*concupiscentia*). While these cities and their respective char-acteristics are distinct, they are as commingled in this present life as the two loves in the conflicted will.[32] Since the Christian (pre-sumably a citizen of Jerusalem)[33] is only a pilgrim here on earth (*en route* to his or her final heavenly residence), he or she is forced to accept his or her natural peace and order (*pax et ordo*); however, it may pale in comparison to God's true peace and order.[34] Since the state is responsible for maintaining this earthly peace and or-der, Augustine contends that there are certain times and condi-tions that require the state to wage war for that end.[35] Yet, in order to preserve even a dim reflection of God's justice,[36] the intentions involved with the violent maintenance of earthly peace must be rightly ordered by God's love.[37]

As morally dramatic and encompassing as it was, the right intention principle was not the last word by Augustine on the topic of just war. In addition to just cause and right intention, Augustine is also credited with the first formulation of the legiti-mate authority principle. Given Augustine's own historical and political milieu, the proper authority to wage war seems vested primarily in the hands of the emperor. In this regard, Augustine is following St. Paul's position in *Romans* 13:1,[38] that all political power stems from God either by command or permission. He thus not only supports the right of sovereigns to wage war, but also supports the obedience of combatants even when serving a sacri-legious prince. Thus, in *Contra Faustum* Augustine states:

> The natural order, which is suited to the peace of mortal things, requires that the authority and deliberation for undertaking war be under the control of a leader [*principem*], and also that, in the executing of military commands, soldiers serve peace and the common well-being. Therefore, a just man, if he should happen to serve as a soldier under a human king who is sacrilegious, could rightly wage a war at the king's com-mand, maintaining the order of civic peace.[39]

This text of Augustine is about the only sure source of the right intention principle; however, *De Libero Arbitrio* does entertain the injustice of private war through the lens of personal self-defense. Augustine concludes that since one's own life is something that can be taken away against one's will,[40] it is not worth killing to preserve it. While this position seems somewhat extreme, it is in keeping with Augustine's logic on the proper end of love (God). Thus, to kill independently of legitimate authority (*i.e.*, for the common good) is to act out of concupiscence.

With the principles of just cause, right intention and legitimate authority, we can clearly see how Augustine has laid the foundation for the subsequent development of just war theory. Like Cicero before him, Augustine also alluded to some of the principles that would later join the full complement, for example, last resort.[41]

In conclusion, one aspect of Augustine's right intention principle that is completely overlooked in contemporary consideration is the historical context in which he conceived this notion. Augustine would certainly have assumed that ultimate sovereign authority and especially with regard to the exercise of prudential judgment would have been vested solely in the emperor (as in the case of the Roman Empire) or in a prince (*principem*.) Theologically speaking, then, since the emperor, the king or the prince would be anointed by the Church and therefore, rule by divine right, it would also have assumed that his "prudential judgment" would have been in sync with his conscience and even with God. This theology of government is entirely different from a secular and democratic one; and, the very notion of prudential judgment of a single individual belongs to such a philosophy, or theology, as the rule and decision of one over the many. In essence, the notion of prudential judgment seems to lose all philosophical credibility when it is applied to a single individual who rules by his own wits and whose authority does not derive from above. Therefore, there is the further problem of the modern assumption of the separation of Church and State, which would be entirely alien to Augustine as well as the Ancient and Medieval worlds.

AUGUSTINE'S INFLUENCE ON MEDIEVAL JUST WAR THOUGHT

Needless to say, Augustine profoundly influenced Medieval just war theology, especially two noteworthy accomplishments: Gratian's compilation of the *Decretum* and St. Thomas Aquinas' treatment of just war in the *Summa Theologiae*. While the canonists who followed Gratian after the Eleventh century continued to develop and refine the theory, the *ad bellum* focus remained within the Augustinian boundaries of just cause, right intention and legitimate authority.[42] In Professor Frederick Russell's seminal work, *The Just War in the Middle Ages*, he is clear and succinct in his comment on Augustine's influence on the great canonist: "The *locus classicus* of texts concerning warfare was the lengthy *Causa* 23. The influence of St. Augustine suffused the entire *Causa*; it would be difficult to fault Gratian for the comprehensiveness of his selection of Augustinian texts."[43]

As Russell further points out, *Causa* 23 is the central document for the consideration and formulation of just war. The document is guided by the concerns and preoccupations of the day: the theological justification of warfare, the Church's authority in waging war, the inherent problems of Christian military service and the issue of the Crusades, for instance. Furthermore, it appears that Gratian's attempt to engage, organize and articulate these problems led to a retrieval and a more thorough reflection on the fundamental Augustinian rubric.

The first Question of *Causa* 23 takes up the problem of whether or not the Gospel allows soldiering. Gratian begins with a list of Scriptural passages that prohibit any kind of violence, citing almost exclusively from the *Gospel of St. Matthew*. In response to these prohibitions, Gratian elicits the help of St. Augustine, briefly summarizing his theology of right intention and supporting the summary with carefully chosen passages from the Bishop's corpus. For example, Gratian juxtaposes Augustine's thoughts on the precepts of patience and their emphasis on interior, moral perfection (*Sermon on the Child of the Centurion*) with his exhortation that the moral soldier fight with an inner disposition of peace (*Letter to Boniface*, 98). Gratian immediately follows these citations with

Augustine's famous passage from *Contra Faustum*[44] that decries only the violence that is rooted in concupiscence and reminds us that St. John the Baptist commanded soldiers to be content with their pay, not to lay down their arms.[45] After allowing Augustine to speak with very little commentary from himself, Gratian concludes Question I in his own words: "From all this we gather that soldiering is not a sin, and that the precepts of patience are to be observed in the preparation of the heart, not in the ostentation of the body."[46]

While Question I dealt specifically with the problem of soldiering, one can see how, at times, its purpose overlaps with that of a theological justification of war itself. However, it is in the second Question of *Causa* 23, that Gratian actually defines just war in close accord with the Ciceronian-Augustinian formula, thus including the reasons of *res repetitis, ulciscuntur iniurias* and the repulsion of enemy attack.[47] The theological effort is taken up again in earnest in Question IV where Gratian attempts to interpret the Gospel injunction on "taking up the sword,"[48] concluding that Christ's meaning referred narrowly to those who fight without legitimate authority.[49] Again, he calls upon the support of Augustine to emphasize the corrective aim of vengeance and how when administered with the proper disposition, it is "really" an expression of mercy. Gratian, however, does not end his theological examination there, for in Question V he revisits the injunction from the *Gospel of St. Matthew* Chapter 26 and combines it with the fifth commandment. To address this, Gratian focuses upon Moses and the case for divine authority in killing and waging war, directly citing *De Civitate Dei* on the guaranteed innocence of those who kill either by divine or political authority.[50] In this way, Gratian successfully provides a theological interpretation of the legitimate authority principle. Hence, by relying primarily upon the Augustinian principles of legitimate authority and right intention, Gratian seems to progress in his goal of providing a thorough and concise theological justification of war.

There is little doubt that the question of the Church's authority to wage war is inherently controversial. Yet, by the time of Gratian, the Medieval period had already built up a store of significant examples of bishops either inciting or simply waging war (*e.g.*, Gregory the Great and Leo IV). This growing precedence must certainly have influenced Gratian's view on the subject, since he includes some of these instances in his analysis of just warfare in *Causa* 23. This is not to say that Gratian arrives at an unequivocal decision about the matter; in fact, his position seems somewhat ambiguous, like the paradoxical state of the bishop who by law may exhort others to war but may not actually wage it under his own authority.[51] However, the ambiguities may be more theoretical than practical when viewed through such historical events as the Crusades, which show the Church exercising what is clearly an illicit power and authority to wage war during the Middle Ages.

While in the end, Gratian's position is ambiguous, he was nevertheless inclined to build an argument in favor of the Church's authority to wage war. Central to his argument is the theological conflation of the ideas of political, ecclesiastical and divine authority. The logical path that leads to this conflation begins with Question III where in two canons Gratian praises the act of killing in defense of country or allies, in effect acknowledging the righteous duty of the state to protect both her own members as well as her friends.[52] Gratian attempted to demonstrate that the Church possesses authority equal to or at least analogous to that of the state, and thus has the right to wage war. To this end, Gratian cites three successive canons in Question V that by implication extend to the Church the state's natural duty to administer vengeance. The first two of these canons attempts to craft a moral legitimacy of killing by duly appointed agents and the Church's responsibility to "defend those who are accused of [this] bloodshed"; that is to say, those who "in the exercise of public power put to death the wicked by the command of the law."[53] By citing the authority of the Old Testament wars, the third canon of this series declares that war waged by God's authority in no wise violates the fifth commandment. When the first two of these canons are read within the context of the third, Gratian's logic concludes that the Church's authority to wage war seems obvious; since the Church is the paramount representative of God, who in his interpretation not only defends publicly authorized killing but, it seems, can also authorize it. Canon 18 furthers Gratian's ludicrous position by confirming the moral legitimacy of state authorized torture, while contriving the insights of St. Augustine to suit his purpose: "While all these things are feared [*i.e.*, the organs of punishment], the wicked are held in check and the good live quietly among the wicked."[54] One might say, however, that for all practical intents, the Church was already led astray by its kindred function with the state in its own relentless war against heresy. But in case the implied link between Church and state authority to exact vengeance is lost on the reader, Gratian explicitly declares the Church's dubious right to exert compulsion upon heretics in the first canon of Question VI: "The Church must compel the wicked to the good, as Christ compelled Paul," to which Gratian adds, "the wicked have to be removed from evil by the lash of tribulations."[55] Thus, Gratian takes the absurd position that the Church, like the state, bears the authority to impose penal evil upon wrongdoers, even to the extent of torture or execution. To round out the rhetorical sequence of Question V on the Church's authority to wage war, Gratian cites the canon granting heavenly residence to those who die fighting the infidel and quotes Pope Nicholas' promise of the same to the Frankish troops.[56]

The logical implications gathered in Questions III, V and VI seem to converge in Question VIII where the most definitive statements on the matter are to be found. Echoing the canons of Question III and V, Gratian places in sequence the canons concerning the pope's responsibility to defend and protect Christians offering the same promise of "heavenly residence" to those who die defending them.[57] The second of these canons identifies explicitly those against whom defense must be made as the "enemies of the holy faith and the adversaries of all religions." This characterization of the enemy seems conveniently adapted to the rising Crusader spirit that arguably began with Leo IV's call to arms against the Saracen invasion of Rome in A.D. 846. It should come as no surprise then when Gratian presents the examples of both Leo IV and Gregory the Great in their respective crusades against the enemies of the faith:

> The prelates of the Church are therefore allowed, following the example of the Blessed Gregory, to call upon the emperor or any generals to defend the faithful. It is even allowed, with the Blessed Leo, vigorously to

exhort anybody to make a defense against the adversaries of the holy
faith and to incite everybody to fend off the violence of the infidels.[58]

In final analysis, however, Gratian's definitive tone here and his
conflation of political, ecclesiastical and divine authority in Questions III, V and VI actually elevated the Church above the secular
powers; for her "exhortations" may certainly have been considered commands seeing that the Church had been invested with
the authority of God whose wars were always *a fortiori* just.
Hence, when the time came for Urban II to call the first Crusade,
there was no secular dissent. That is not to suggest that there was
no subsequent dissent, for Gratian's word on just warfare was
certainly not the last on the subject. Although *Causa* 23 gathered
together some of the important canons and commentary on just
warfare, it was not exactly a tightly compact argument. On the
contrary, the treatment was sketchy, commencing in fits and
starts, rather than flowing coherently from well established
premises to definitive conclusions.

While many of Gratian's successors would attempt to bring
more clarity and order to the theory, it was St. Thomas Aquinas in
the thirteenth century who brought about the most systematic articulation of just war theory by returning directly to St.
Augustine's works. Aquinas' contribution to the just war tradition
was not so much additive as it was systematic; he did not discover
any new principles to the theory, but he did gather the previously
scattered treatments into a systematic presentation. None of his
predecessors had arranged their insights into such a coherent and
determinate theory as he. In this way, Aquinas may be considered
the second founder of just war theory.

Remarkably, St. Thomas Aquinas condensed the whole of *ad
bellum* just war theory into a single *quodlibet*: "Whether it is always
sinful to wage war?"[59] The framing of this question leaves little
doubt that Aquinas sought a sound *theological* solution; and in
doing so, he relied almost entirely upon Augustine in his *responsum*. In short, Augustine's original insights provided St. Thomas
Aquinas with all he needed for his *sed contra*:

Augustine says in a sermon on the son of the centurion: If the Christian
Religion forbade war altogether, those who sought salutary advice in

the Gospel would rather have been counseled to cast aside their arms, and to give up soldiering altogether. On the contrary, they were told: "Do violence to no man; and be content with your pay." If he commanded them to be content with their pay, he did not forbid soldiering.[60]

This argument provides one of the few, if only, Gospel passages that suggests a moral tolerance of war. This passage is, however, problematic on at least two counts: first, the citation itself from the *Gospel of St. Luke* relates the words of St. John the Baptist, and *not* Jesus; second, the passage is somewhat vague, requiring the reader to make his or her own deduction as to whether or not the Baptist's words are at all directed to the moral question of war. Hence, Aquinas' *responsum* incorporates Augustine's three principles (legitimate authority, just cause and right intent) into a supportive argument, inferring from them that war can be just and thus deemed morally acceptable to the Christian religion. Beginning with legitimate authority, Aquinas synthesizes the Augustinian principle with the Aristotelian notion of the common good:[61]

> For it is not the business of a private individual to declare war . . . Moreover, it is not the business of a private individual to summon together the people, which has to be done in wartime. And as the care of the common weal is committed to those who are in authority, it is their business to watch over the common weal of the city, kingdom or province subject to them.[62]

Combining this natural idea of the common good with the uniquely Christian take on political authority, Aquinas cites St. Paul to relate the state's analogous duty of vengeance with its responsibility to protect against foreign attack:

> And just as it is lawful for them to have recourse to the sword in defending that common weal against internal disturbances, when they punish evil doers, according to the words of the Apostle (*Romans* xiii, 4) . . . so too, it is their business to have recourse to the sword of war in defending the common weal against external enemies.[63]

From the analogy drawn between domestic and foreign disturbance, St. Thomas moves to the exhortative conclusion found in

Psalm LXXXI, 4: "Hence it is said to those in authority, Rescue the poor: and deliver the needy out of the hand of the sinner."[64] This conclusion carries a very strong theological message in suggesting that the fundamental duty of legitimate authority bears a close resemblance to the corporal works of mercy. Relatedly, Aquinas' reply to the first objection recalls Augustine's interpretation of the violator of Christ's proscription against taking up the sword as one who fights without proper authority. Thus, in completing the link between the pagan and Christian rationales, Aquinas offers Augustine's own articulation of the legitimacy principle as the final conclusion:

> And for this reason Augustine says [in *Contra Faustum* xxii.75] the natural order conducive to peace among mortals demands that the power to declare and counsel war should be in the hands of those who hold the supreme authority.[65]

With this quotation from Augustine, Aquinas resolves his treatment of legitimate authority. Yet, the particular characteristics distinguishing legitimate from illegitimate authority are never addressed. He does, however, list three types of political organization (*civitas, regnum, provincia*) that at least correspond with the emerging political landscape of his day; that is, the growing consolidation of kingdoms that foreran the modern nation-states.[66] For the most part, legitimate authority rested in the sovereign (*princeps*) and his or her duly appointed officials.[67] Having demonstrated the necessity of legitimate authority in just warfare, Aquinas moved to the principle of just cause. Unlike his previous treatment of the legitimacy principle, just cause is not argued but merely explained. In what appears to be a rather extreme attention to brevity, Aquinas merely states that a hostile attack must be made upon a "deserving" recipient (*mereantur*). Again, he relies upon St. Augustine to precise this principle:

> Wherefore Augustine says (*QQ. In Hept., qu.X, super Jos*): A just war is wont to be described as one that avenges wrongs, when a nation or state has to be punished, for refusing to make amends for the wrongs inflicted by its subjects, or to restore what is has seized unjustly.[68]

The stark dependency on Augustine shines through again with this reference to the famous *"ulciscuntur injurias"* (avenging injuries) formula for just cause. Other than this citation, the *responsum* contains no further elaboration on the principle. The only other reference to it is made in his third reply where he cites Augustine again on the peaceful end of all just wars.

Aquinas thus moves quickly to the final principle of right intention, and again relies entirely upon Augustine's insights, citing the often-quoted passage from *Contra Faustum* XXII, 74, warning against any violence inspired by concupiscence. After all, it was Augustine who made the ingenious shift from hatred to love in grounding the moral disposition of the just Christian warrior. Whereas, the primary concern of the canonists was to construe charity somehow as the legal grounds for warfare by the Church or a Christian prince, St. Thomas Aquinas sought to restore the theological integrity of the just war principles by relying upon the authority of sacred Scripture and the insights of St. Augustine.

The brevity of St. Thomas Aquinas' treatment of war is in part due to his unique dialectical approach; however, it is another feature of this same approach that relevant insights can be culled from other questions in the *Summa Theologiae*. For example, his treatment of vengeance casts some prefatory light on the concept of legitimate authority;[69] his question on murder touches upon the later developed principle of proportionality through the caption of self-defense.[70] The organization of these questions allows the reader to cross-reference related discussions for the sake of clarification and comprehension. But what is of greater interest than this branching dialectic is the overall context in which the topic of war is discussed, that is within the scope of charity. By establishing the discussion on war within the context of God's love, Aquinas reveals his *true* Augustinian character. Not only has Aquinas relied heavily upon Augustine's insights (*i.e.*, in crafting the entire rubric), but also he co-opted the more important universal theme of charity as the essential means of justifying warfare. Nevertheless, it is noteworthy to mention that St. Thomas Aquinas' treatment of war is situated within his discussion of some of the more heinous of vices in accordance with his Augustinian theology of sin: it seems that the Angelic Doctor wants us to remember that war carries with it the plague of sin.[71] Despite Aquinas' departure from Augustine on the question of whether war is always sinful,[72] his rhetorical organization of this important question of war between questions on *"hatred," "sloth," "envy," "discord," "strife," "sedition"* and *"scandal"* strongly appears to disclose a profound hermeneutical insight—perhaps, St. Thomas himself knows that his argumentation does not quite jive with the saintly Bishop of Hippo whom he greatly admired?[73]

AUGUSTINE'S INFLUENCE ON EARLY MODERN THOUGHT

Through St. Thomas' systematic treatment of war, the Augustinian imprint is boldly italicized, preserving an Ancient schema for subsequent theorists during the Renaissance and Modernity. Some of the chief contributors during this time retain the Augustinian blueprint; thinkers like de Vitoria and Suárez of the Salamancan School and the Reformist Grotius will take on the problem of just warfare from a more legalistic perspective, placing greater emphasis on the *jus gentium*, while leaving nearly intact the Augustinian legacy passed on by Aquinas.

Among the Modern just war theorists, the three paragons whose imprint emboldens the margins of the central Augustinian-Thomistic rubric are the Spanish Domincan Francisco de Vitoria, the Spanish Jesuit Francisco Suárez and the Dutch Protestant Hugo Grotius.[74] Vitoria and Suárez were integral in the revival of Thomistic thought that was spreading throughout the Catholic centers of learning in Sixteenth and Seventeenth century Europe, ostensibly in response to the Protestant Reformation. In fact, Vitoria is credited with founding one of the most important schools in this revival, the renowned school of Salamanca. Although Grotius was a Reform thinker, he paid serious intellectual deference to both the Augustinian-Thomistic just war tradition and to Vitoria and Suárez as the true pioneers of international law.[75] The precise point of their conceptual intersection, however, can be found in their reliance upon the surety of both natural and divine law in relation to just war theory.

Nearly all scholars agree that the major contributions of Vitoria, Suárez and Grotius fall within the context of international relations; yet, it is precisely within the parameters of the *jus gentium* that a fuller, more refined development of the just war principles were undertaken. As a result, the three thinkers brought a greater depth to the theory, adding new principles that not only increased the total number but also necessitated their distinction into the categories of *ad bellum* and *in bello*.[76] All three thinkers move from the Augustinian and Thomistic foundation in just war theory, adding their own respective social, geopolitical conditions and circumstances.[77]

Francisco de Vitoria (1483-1546) followed a fundamentally Thomistic methodology in formulating his view of just warfare, outlining in detail the fruits of his speculation in both *De indis* and *De jure belli*. The geopolitical circumstances under which he considered the idea of just warfare were at least twofold: the Spanish colonization of the Americas and the developing divisions within Christianity. Arguably the most influential event on Vitoria's just war thinking was the Spanish expansion in the New World. From the oppressive and violent treatment of the native Americans by the Conquistadors to the Spanish Crown's claims of conquest over the New World, Vitoria found a wealth of moral reasons to re-evaluate the rights and limitations of war. While his *lectio* on the native American peoples (*De indis*) deals explicitly with these issues, his follow-up *lectio De jure belli* gives a brief but comprehensive analysis of *ad bellum* just war principles.

In *De jure belli*, Vitoria outlines his treatment of war within four questions, only three of which will be of present interest since the last deals exclusively with *in bello* considerations: Whether it is ever lawful for Christians to wage war? On whose authority war may be waged? What are the causes of just war? What Christians may lawfully do against enemies? The first question is an Ancient one addressing the pacifist contention against any and all violence, and Vitoria answers with the usual Augustinian-Thomistic retorts. However, he does add a very interesting summary insight concerning the practical relationship between the natural and divine laws:

> But the Gospel law forbids nothing, which is allowed by natural law.
> Therefore, what was lawful under natural law and in the written law
> [*i.e.*, Divine law] is no less lawful under the Gospel law.[78]

By uniting the so-called Old and New divine laws, Vitoria successfully vindicates the natural law as an unimpeachable organ of
Christian moral logic.[79] Thus, Vitoria applies natural law principles to the new global question of justifying war both for the security and happiness of the world:

> But there can be no security in the State unless enemies are made to de-
> sist from wrong by the fear of war. . .For there would be no condition of
> happiness for the world, nay, its condition would be one of utter mis-
> ery, if oppressors and robbers and plunderers could with impunity
> commit their crimes and oppress the good and innocent.[80]

Following the Augustinian principle on the question of
authority, he brings some added nuance to the topic, carrying
over a distinction he made in the previous question between "defensive" and "offensive" wars.[81] For example, he argues that in the
case of defensive war–which must be constituted by the perception of immediate danger–any private person bears the authority
to resist violence with violence (*vim ui repellere licet*).[82] This resis-
tance applies to both the defense of one's person as well as one's
property, the latter allowable only if an interval of time has not
lapsed between the initial robbery and the subsequent recovery
(*incontinenti*).[83] Now, in the case of offensive war, only commonwealths have the authority to wage war, presumably for the purpose of vengeance and restoration and thus requiring no
immediacy in response. Of course, commonwealths are able to
wage both kinds of war, but private persons only the defensive
type.

Vitoria's idea of the commonwealth relies upon the Aristote-
lian-Thomistic notion of a "perfect community."[84] And in accordance with Augustine,[85] he includes the prince as bearing this
same authority to wage war inasmuch as the prince is the formal
cause of civil authority in the commonwealth.[86] In recognizing the
ambiguity of sovereign authority (a problem that persists even today), de Vitoria focuses on the problem of determining the various and often overlapping powers of the emperor, monarchs and

other princes. Using the example of those princes who governed over "perfect communities" yet owed fealty to the emperor, Vitoria makes the decision to attribute to them the full authority to wage war without the emperor's approval. On the other hand, Vitoria speculates that those princes whose political jurisdiction did not extend over a definitive commonwealth did not have the authority to wage war. Vitoria admits in the end that such particular matters of authority are ultimately fleshed out by human law and the *jus gentium*, allowing custom and circumstance to have the final say on the matter.

Vitoria's nuances on legitimate authority notwithstanding, his detailed investigation into the just causes of war result in his more significant contributions to the theory. At first, he retraces the steps laid out by Augustine's *ulciscuntur injurias*, adding the explicit right of self-defense mentioned previously in his reply to the first question. Vitoria emphasizes the necessity of an attack or injury and thus declares on the authority of Augustine that "it is clear that we may not turn our sword against those who do us no harm, the killing of the innocent being forbidden by natural law."[87] Moreover, he includes as just causes both property recovery (*recuperatio rerum*) following Cicero and punishment (*punitio*) following the lead of Augustine.[88]

Within the context of attack and injury, however, Vitoria brings to light a newly revised *ad bellum* principle of proportionality, for he states, "Not every kind and degree of wrong can suffice for commencing a war."[89] He goes on to explain that vengeance and punishment should not be inordinate but should befit the nature and degree of the crime. There are even cases when an unjust attack should go unanswered due to the potential disproportion of injury and carnage a war may produce. Vitoria applies this principle not only to the enemy, but also to the commonwealth, considering retaliatory attack insofar as their good gained may be exceeded by the evil endured.[90]

Vitoria's extensive examination of just causes led him to consider a perennial and what many might consider a controversial issue in his discussion of comparative justice. Contrary to Augustine's own position that assumes there must be one party that is good and another that is evil, de Vitoria seems to appreciate the ambiguity in such moral determinations. In which case, according to Augustine at least, this problem would be contradictory because rival combatants would both possess a just cause for war. For Vitoria, the conundrum inherent in this principle is solved equivocally: on the one hand, the principle itself is contradictory since the assumption of justice on both sides leads to the fact that both combatants are attacking innocents, which clearly violates the natural law. On the other hand, Vitoria acknowledges the ethical condition of "invincible ignorance," thus allowing that either one or both combatants are so ignorant of their own cause that they are both exonerated from violating the just cause principle.

As a fit ending to his treatment on just war, Vitoria includes an explicit preponderance of peace in his final section of the *De jure belli*, thus identifying the *ad bellum* principle of last resort. In elucidating this admonitory principle he reveals the Augustinian vision of love as the arch-principle circumscribing the entire *modus cogitationis* concerning just war theory:

> All this can be summarized in a few canons or rules of warfare. First canon: Assuming that a prince has authority to make war, he should first of all not go seeking occasions and causes of war, but should, if possible, live in peace with all men, as St. Paul enjoins on us. Moreover, he should reflect that others are his neighbors, whom we are bound to love as ourselves, and that we all have one common Lord, before whose tribunal we shall have to render our account. For it is the extreme of savagery to seek for and rejoice in grounds for killing and destroying men whom God has created and for whom Christ died. But only under compulsion and reluctantly should he come to the necessity of war.[91]

Perhaps the most notable thinkers of the Salamancan School was Francisco Suárez (1548-1617). While his charisma and teaching prowess reputedly paled in comparison to Vitoria's, his comprehensive mastery of the Thomistic method and his profound influence on the revival of Scholasticism continue to secure his rank as one of the greatest thinkers of his time.[92] Unlike the glaring contributions he made to such topics as metaphysics and epistemology, Suárez modeled much of his political thought directly upon the teachings of Vitoria.[93] Like Vitoria, Suárez outlined his speculation according to the four questions of whether, by whom, when and how just wars may be fought.[94] Moreover, like his master, he provides a more detailed prescription of just causes fitted to his own historical circumstances.

Suárez, too, seems to accept the Augustinian-Thomistic triplex of just war conditions; however, the principle of right intention is not explicitly mentioned. Instead, Suárez attaches the principle of proportionality, stating:

> First, the war must be undertaken by a legitimate power; second, it must have a just cause; and third, it must be carried out in a proper manner, with due proportion observed at its beginning, during its prosecution, and at victory.[95]

The principle of proportionality mentioned here is not the *ad bellum* type, but represents more of how war is to be waged (*in bello*). His ostensible replacement of the traditional right intention principle does not necessarily result in its discharge, but there certainly appears to be a shift in emphasis towards *in bello* concerns, probably brought about by the increasing technology of warfare in Suárez's time and its expanded use in Spain's colonization efforts.

Concerning the Christian moral problem with war, Suárez phrases the question a bit differently from Vitoria. Rather than ask whether it is lawful for Christians to wage war, he asks explicitly whether war is intrinsically evil? He answers this question with a resounding "no" in a misguided effort to follow an Augustinian logic of love, *ad bellum* proportionality and last resort:

> One may add that war is opposed to peace, to love of one's enemies, and to the forgiveness of injuries. . .to [which] Augustine replies [*De Civitate Dei* XIX, 7] that he deems it advisable to avoid war in so far as is possible, and to undertake it only in cases of extreme necessity, when no alternative remains, but he also holds that war is not entirely evil, since the fact that evils follow upon war is incidental, and since greater evils would result if war were never allowed. . .Similarly, love is not opposed to the love of one's enemies; for whoever wages war honorably, hates not individuals, but actions which are justly punished.[96]

Here, Suárez is clearly manipulating Augustine's theology of love in his desire to justify warfare reminiscent of Gratian's earlier rationalizations. This method of picking and choosing from Augustine contradicts the spirit of his thought rooted in the Gospel exhortation of penance and interior conversion, something assumed in his reference to the sovereign's intentions for waging war. What Suárez appears to easily overlook is just how terrible a decision this is according to Augustine. Suárez's questionable use of love also suggests to the reader a possible reason for his decision to leave the principle of right intention unspoken; for so long as the precepts of charity are not perceived to be violated by just warfare, there is no need to delve further into the motives of a sovereign whose cause is apparently just. This shrewd type of argumentation is certainly in keeping with what was the early polemical obsession of the Jesuits in their confrontation with the Reformers; and thus, Suárez would have been accustomed to finding and using important Christian sources like Augustine in order to justify his positions.[97]

On the principle of legitimate authority, Suárez agrees with Vitoria that all citizens have the right of self-defense; hence, he will relegate his treatment of this principle to offensive wars, which can only be waged by leaders of a "perfect community."[98] As with Vitoria, the prince has full authority to wage war;[99] however, in the case of a "negligent" sovereign, the commonwealth may "take vengeance on the prince, depriving him of his authority."[100] While Vitoria included the possibility of revolution in his political philosophy, Suárez seems to have rhetorically "upped the *ante*," so to speak, by being so explicit and at the same time so vague about what justifies revolt. Otherwise, he and Vitoria are of identical mind on this issue, both acknowledging a primacy of the commonwealth over any particular prince.[101] In his concluding statements on legitimate authority, Suárez connects the principle with love, demonstrating again the encompassing reach the Augustinian application extends over the Christian mindset of just warfare: "I hold that when a war is declared without legitimate authority, it is contrary not only to charity, but also to justice, even if a legitimate cause exists."[102]

Although there were some points of divergence with regard to particular application, Suárez agreed with his predecessor on the general principles of just cause.[103] Both thinkers gave comprehensive, practical treatment of the principle in line with their own historic-political context. With the exception of religious wars, both derive particular just causes from the natural law; in fact, Suárez entitles his question on just cause, "What is a Just Title for War, on the Basis of Natural Reason?"[104] Again, like Vitoria, in the case of just causes, Suárez gives a circumstantial precedence to human law in the form of the *jus gentium*. Thus, the laws that govern international respect of property, national boundaries, peace and commercial agreements and even the waging of just wars fall under the customs and obligations designated by human will and ingenuity, not by compulsion of the natural law.[105] Suárez, however, did reaffirm and thus preserve a substantial dependency upon the natural law for good human legislation.[106]

Working within the general notion of vengeance, Suárez lists the kinds of injuries and corresponding retributions that constitute just cause. Although his list appears more detailed and prolonged, he outlines the same basic criteria as Vitoria, *i.e.*, defense, recuperation of property and punishment.[107] Also for Suárez, the principle of proportionality held the same sway over just cause as it did for Vitoria, precluding a hostile attack (either defensive or offensive) if the damages outweighed the rewards of victory.[108] This reasoning on proportionality led Suárez to include the related principle of likelihood of success, for which he provided a specified guide or formula for evaluating and determining such likelihood based upon acceptable degrees of certainty and doubt.[109] This process of evaluation, coupled with Suárez's requirement that the prince seek good war counsel, placed the determination of war squarely within the sovereign's own realm of prudential judgment. However, unlike Vitoria, Suárez granted a more juridical quality to the sovereign's power of determination, recognizing the prince who wages war as both a judge and prosecutor of vindictive justice.[110] Suárez thus opens the door for a more modern, realistic view of the sovereign's right to wage war.

While Suárez's treatment of the likelihood principle represented one of the more detailed advances beyond that of his predecessors, the proportionality principle stood as a kind of keystone for the entire *ad bellum* structure. And yet, the textual evidence of this binding role once again implicates the Augustinian principle of love as the true, master-criterion of the just war theory:

> If one prince begins a war upon another, even with just cause, while exposing his own realm to disproportionate loss and peril, then he will be sinning not only against charity, but also against justice.[111]

If Vitoria and Suárez can be regarded as the pioneers of international law, then Hugo Grotius (1583-1646) would be the first settler. He followed with great sympathy and methodological imitation the Thomistic precision of the Salamancan School.[112] And, although he is often credited as the father of secular political theory, his analysis of just war in *De jure belli ac pacis* is replete with biblical and patristic arguments, exhibiting as much acumen in theology as in law or politics. However, his major appeal in justifying war was made to the authority of law; for his efforts to articulate a rationale for just warfare focused less on the general principles (about which he was in fundamental agreement with his predecessors), than on the particular legalities inherent in the combatants' disputed claims on justice. Hence, Grotius made most of his contribution to just war theory in his exhaustive treatment of the principle of just cause.

In the case of war, Grotius preferred to see justice through the prism of law as evidenced in his principle treatment of natural law in *De jure belli ac pacis*.[113] For Grotius, the pillars of justice were contained in the natural and divine laws, both of which are immutable and universally binding on all persons.[114] Like Vitoria and Suárez before him, he invested a profound trust in the natural law; and given its proper correlation and application to the determination of human laws, this trust was logically extended to the law of nations and the principles of just warfare.[115] Moreover, Grotius conceived wars as fundamentally analogous to lawsuits, for he writes, "The grounds of war are as numerous as those of judicial actions. For where the power of law ceases, there war begins."[116] It was this emphasis on law that enabled Grotius to offer the first real systematization of just war theory predominantly along juridical lines.[117]

For the general criteria of just cause, Grotius also relied upon Augustine's ubiquitous *ulciscuntur injurias*. He also accepted the three generic causes of defense, recovery of property and punish-ment; but to these three he added a forth cause of debt collection, perhaps an addition inspired by his legal preoccupations.[118] He upheld the individual's right to self-defense (accepting the condi-tion of immediate danger), but adamantly objected against the right of the people to overthrow a sovereign.[119] Coming out of the Roman legal tradition, the right to self-defense included property and could be exercised by private citizens and states alike; how-ever, the individual's recovery of property had to constitute an immediate response, otherwise it was deemed an offensive ac-tion.[120] Regarding punishment, Grotius detracted from his prede-cessors (especially Suárez) when he extended the sovereign's right to punish any transgression of the natural law anywhere in the world.[121] This expansion of the right to punish, which was tradi-tionally restricted to injuries incurred by a sovereign's own peo-ple, allies or the property within his own borders, surely ushered in the Modern problem of wars waged on the grounds of either fraternal or humanitarian intervention.

Grotius' examination of just cause criteria was voluminous and, at times, atomistic. It included such particular considerations as what kinds of objects could be reduced to property (e.g. geo-graphic entities like rivers and seas, natural resources),[122] the right to use another's property so long as the owner suffered no loss,[123] free passage and even settlement for refugees,[124] free access to trade routes, free passage to escape or pursue an enemy during war.[125] Each specific issue is given a thorough legal analysis to as-certain whether or not an injury has been suffered to such an ex-tent that war is a just recourse for vengeance or restitution, a monumental attempt at discovering every just and unjust cause of warfare in the seventeenth century world.

The *ad bellum* principles of proportionality and likelihood of success also played an important part of Grotius' idea of just war. In fact, the danger of defeat, excessive damage and hardship led him to hold a very high threshold of anticipated success based upon a sure presumption of superiority: "For to avenge a wrong, or to assert a right by force of arms requires a superiority of strength."[126] These principles were so important that they led Grotius to a general presumption against war, in spite of his meticulous examination into just causes. To articulate this presumption, he, like so many before him, called upon the father of just war theory: "This is what Augustine used to say, that war ought not to be undertaken save when the hope of gain was shown to be greater than the fear of loss;"[127] and elsewhere Grotius carries the same line of reasoning to its final, peace-seeking conclusion: "Now war is of the utmost importance, seeing that in consequence of war most sufferings usually fall also upon innocent persons. Therefore, in the midst of divergent opinions we must lean towards peace."[128]

A WORD ON THE CONTEMPORARY DISCUSSION

For the most part, from the Eighteenth century to the middle of the Twentieth century, there is little interest in just war theory especially since the great European powers at the time were preoccupied with expanding the boundaries and influence of their respective nation-states. In fact, it is not until the Second World War and the dreadful American decision to drop the atomic bomb on Japan that the world begins to question these matters once again. Then, as the cold war emerges in the 1950's, the question of just warfare becomes intertwined with the struggle between the democratic United States and the totalitarian Soviet Union. But, the question of just war is addressed once again with a renewed passion by the largest gathering of the world's bishops at the Second Vatican Council in Rome during the 1960's when the Council Fathers began to focus their attention on the moral depravity of war and its deplorable consequences on the poor, the disenfranchised and the necessity of peace. Finally, in 1994, Pope John Paul II's new *Catechism of the Catholic Church* appeared and recharged the discussion of just war theory with its new insights concerning the Augustinian presumption of peace.

CONCLUSION: "BLESSED ARE THE PEACEMAKERS"

Alas, despite its earnest attempts at reconciling what amounts to the disparity between the Gospel and the exigencies of the world, the entire history of Christian just war theory is a mere compromise that has often fallen to contradiction and convenient rationale in its defense of the very primitive vice of the lust for power. Let us recall that the early Christian Fathers—and, indeed, as the Orthodox tradition continues to maintain—simply could not see any compatibility between the sin of war and the Christian *ethos*. It seems that we have also forgotten that Augustine's own speculations on the rightness and wrongness of warfare are *questions for conscience* that are not a theory really, but pastoral considerations that belong to his theology of love in its aspirations for a kingdom of peace. Now, this is not to say that the just war theory that derives from St. Augustine's speculation is entirely useless, but that the theory, and more importantly the theorists, must remember its commitment to the mystical prescription of Jesus in the *Gospel of St. Matthew*, where he instructs the faithful to move beyond justice to charity, and beyond vengeance to radical forgiveness. Despite what some contemporary theorists have to say, any authentic claim to the Augustinian tradition would have to involve a strong *presumption of peace* as evident in all of the major contributors to the development of the theory. After all, the Augustinian just war theory that develops in the West, for better or ill, belongs to Christianity; and therefore, it must confront the ambiguity it suffers in deriving from a heritage that is founded on the precepts of love. In citing *"Gaudium et Spes"* from the documents of the Second Vatican Council, the *Catechism of the Catholic Church* eloquently exhorts: "The fifth commandment forbids the intentional destruction of human life. Because of the evils and injustices that accompany all war, the Church insistently urges everyone to prayer and to action so that the divine Goodness may free us from the Ancient bondage of war."[129]

Notes

1 For example Thucydides' *Melian Dialogue* which presents a discussion on war between the Athenians and Melians; and Plato's *Laws* 1, 628 where he touches upon the presumption against war and the end of war as being peace and friendship.

[2] Cf. Frederick Russell, *The Just War in the Middle Ages* (Cambridge: Cambridge University Press, 1975), 3, where in his comprehensive history, Russell claims that Aristotle is the first, in fact, to coin the term "just war."

[3] *Politics* VII, 15. 1334a 15-16. The translation is by Benjamin Jowett, *The Basic Works of Aristotle*, ed. Richard McKeon (New York: Random House, 1941).

[4] *Ibid.*, VII, 14. 1333b 38-40 and 1334a 1-4.

[5] *De Officiis* I, 35. All of the Latin and English passages of *De Officiis* used in this chapter are taken from Walter Miller's translation in the *Loeb Classic Library*, ed. T.E. Page and W.H.D. Rouse (London: Macmillan Company, 1913).

[6] Cf. also *De Republica* III, 34 where Cicero speaks of just cause as retribution and repelling attackers (*ulciscendi aut propulsandorum hostium causa*).

[7] *Ibid.*, I, 33. It may be contested that when Cicero mentions (*ulciscendi et puniendi*) in the final lines of I, 33, he refers only to a general idea of retribution and punishment, not necessarily as it applies to war. However, in his commentary on Cicero's *De Officiis*, Andrew Roy Dyck provides the following insight: "The general principle announced at the onset of the discussion (*est enim ulciscendi et puniendi modus*) surely applies throughout. For instance, the circumstances in which war can be undertaken, the goal of warfare and the *justitia in hostem* represent application[s] of this general principle to the special circumstances of war." *A Commentary on Cicero, De Officiis* (Ann Arbor: University of Michigan Press, 1996), 134.

[8] *Ibid.*, I, 36. Cicero admits the already established precedent requiring a declaration of war and cites the Roman Fetial Laws as his source. According to Frederick Russell (*The Just War in the Middle Ages*, 6), the proper form of declaration required a list of grievances to be redressed (*res repetitio*). Hence, the *res repetitio* implies the just cause of war interpreted as *ulciscendi et puniendi — a quibus iniuriam acceperis*.

[9] *Ibid.*, I, 38. Cf. Richard Sorabji, "Just War from Ancient Origins to the Conquistadors Debate and its Modern Relevance" in *The Ethics of War*, ed. Richard Sorabji and David Rodin (Burlington: Ashgate Publishing Company, 2006), 27, n.5.

[10] *De Officiis* I, 62. Also III, 29. The preclusion of private war also touches upon the later Legitimate Authority principle.

[11] One could also include here the likelihood of success principle, since it is so closely related to proportionality. On the issue of the conflation of these two principles and Cicero's influence on last resort, cf. Coppieters, Apressyan, Ceulemans, "Last Resort" and Coppieters, Fotion, "Likelihood of Success" in *Moral Constraints on War: Principles and Cases* (New York: Lexington Books, 2002), 101, 79 respectively.

[12] *De Officiis* I, 34.

[13] See also *De Officiis* I, 83 where he comes awfully close to rendering the modern princple of proportionality: "Only a madman, who, in a calm, would pray for a storm; a wise man's way is, when the storm does come, to withstand it with all the means at his command, and especially, when the advantages to be expected

in case of a successful issue are greater than the hazards of the struggle (*Quare in tranquillo tempestatem adversam optare dementis est, subvenire autem tempestati quavis ratione sapientis, eoque magis, si plus adipiscare re explicata boni quam addubitata mali)."Ibid.*, I, 89.

[14] *De Officiis* I, 34.

[15] *Ibid.,* I, 65.

[16] *Ibid.,* I, 74.

[17] Predicating a presumption against war to Cicero may find some detractors among contemporary just war theorists. For example, see James Turner Johnson's article "Just War, As It Was and Is" in *First Things* (January 2005), 15 where he seems to argue that a return to the "classic form" of the just war tradition would rescue it from the recently emerging "Catholic peace tradition," which according to Johnson has made "a case for pacifism for Catholic laity."

[18] Cf. William Stevenson, Jr., *Christian Love and Just War: Moral Paradox and Political Life in St. Augustine and His Modern Interpreters* (Macon: Mercer University Press, 1987), 4. Cf. also Frederick Russell, *Just War in the Middle Ages*, 16. Cf. also Michael Walzer, *Arguing About War* (New Haven: Yale University Press, 2004), 3 and Cf. *The Ethics of War: Classic and Contemporary Readings*, ed. Gregory Reichberg, Henrik Syse and Endre Begby (Malden, MA: Blackwell Publishing, 2006), 70.

[19] Cf. Stevenson, *Christian Love and Just War*, 5. Some scholars have argued that a principle motivation for Augustine's so-called realism on just war was to reconcile the pacifistic Scriptural references found in the New Testament and the early Patristic pacifism of those like Origen and Tertullian with both the Empire's need to defend against the disruption of the *pax Romana Christiana* (brought about by Constantine) and the Church's need to defend against violent heresies like that of the Donatist (implying also that wars can be justly fought on religious grounds). This point is strongly suggested by Frederick Russell in *The Just War in the Middle Ages*, 16. Also cf. Fotion, Coppieters and Apressyan in their introduction to *Moral Constraints on War*, 11. Also cf. Brian Orend, *The Morality of War* (Peterborough: Broadview Press, 1971), 13 and Michael Walzer, *Arguing About War*, 3. For an analysis of Origen's and Tertullian's pacifistic stances against war cf. Adolf Harnack, *Militia Christi: The Christian Religion and the Military in the First Three Centuries*, trans. David McInnes Gracie (Philadelphia: Fortress Press, 1981), 83-86.

[20] *De Civitate Dei* XIX, 14.

[21] *Quaestionum in Heptateuchum* VI, 10, P.L. 34, 547-824: "*Justa autem bella definiri solent, quae ulciscuntur injurias.*" In English, perhaps: "Those wars, moreover, that are defined as just are those which usually avenge injuries." (The translation is ours.) Augustine also agrees with Cicero on the end of war as peace (Cf. *Letter 189 to Boniface*).

[22]Cf. Oliver O'Donovan, *The Just War Revisited* (Cambridge: Cambridge University Press, 2003), 18.

[23] See *De Civitate Dei* XIX, 16: "Hence the duty of anyone who would be blameless includes not only doing no harm to anyone but also restraining a man from sin or punishing his sin, so that either the man who is chastised may be corrected by his experience, or others may be deterred by his example." The translator is Henry Bettenson, *City of God* (London: Penguin Books, 1972), 876. Here again, as in the case with Cicero, one can safely apply this general principle to the specific circumstances of war. Also cf. *Contra Faustum* XXII, 74.

[24] *Contra Faustum* XXII, 74. This translation comes from Michael W. Tkacz and Douglas Kries in *Augustine: Political Writings*, ed. Ernest L. Fortin and Douglas Kries (Indianapolis: Hackett, 1994), 221 by way of *The Ethics of War*, ed. Reichberg, Syse and Begby.

[25] Hating the sin and not the sinner.

[26] Augustine's position on war with respect to his just war theory is equivocal since he can be considered a realist, on the one hand, in as much as he understands war to be at times a "necessary evil"; yet, on the other hand, his position on the conduct of warfare is clearly idealistic because his ideas first of all derive from his faith and, secondly, in his demand that Christian rulers be ruled themselves by love that is none other than God Himself.

[27] Augustine often uses these terms interchangeably throughout his works. Cf. *De Civitate Dei* XIV, 7 and *De Libero Arbitrio* I, 3-4.

[28] *Sermons on the First Letter of St. John, sermon* 7: "Love and do as you will (*Dilige et quod vis fac*)."

[29] For Augustine, the universal good is desired by all; hence he writes in *Confessiones* I, "*Inquietum est cor nostrum donec requiescat in te.*"

[30] *De Civitate Dei* X, 14.

[31] *De Civitate Dei* XV, 4.

[32] For more on Augustine's notion of confusion and ambiguity, see Craig J. N. de Paulo's article "St. Augustine's Phenomenology of Confusion" in *Ambiguity in the Western Mind* (New York: Peter Lang Publishing, 2006.)

[33] *Letter 189 to Boniface*: "Yet, because it is necessary in this world that the citizens of the kingdom of heaven are troubled by temptations among the erring and impious." This translation comes from Louis J. Swift in his edited work *The Early Fathers on War and Military Service* (Wilmington, Michael Glazier, 1983), 118 by way of *The Ethics of War: Classic and Contemporary Readings*.

[34] *De Civitate* XIX, 17.

[35] *De Civitate* XV, 4.

[36] For Augustine there is a great disparity between the true justice of God and the earthly justice of humankind. For an interesting application of this disparity to just war theory, see Stevenson's *Christian Love and Just War*, 118.

[37] *Letter 138 to Marcellinus*: "If the earthly city observes Christian principles, even its wars will be waged with the benevolent purpose that better provision might be made for the defeated to live harmoniously together in justice and godliness. *Ibid.*, Louis J. Swift, *The Early Fathers on War and Military Service*.

[38] See also *Romans* 13:4.

[39] *Contra Faustum* XXII, 75. Fortin and Kries, *Augustine: Political Writings*, 222-3, 225-6 taken from *The Ethics of War: Classic and Contemporary Readings*.

[40] *De Libero Arbitrio* I, 4-5.

[41] Cf. Stevenson, *Christian Love and Just War*, 40.

[42] *The Just War in the Middle Ages*, 86-214. Russell gives a thorough and comprehensive analysis of this development, dividing the contributors between the Decretists and Decretalists.

[43] *Ibid.*, 56.

[44] *Contra Faustum* XXII, 74.

[45] *Gospel of St. Luke* 3:14.

[46] *Causa* 23, q. I, can. 4. Translation by Peter Haggenmacher and Robert Andrews, from the edition of Emil Friedberg, *Decretum Magistri Gratiani*, in *Corpus Iuris Canonici, pars prior* (Leipzig: Tauchniz, 1879), taken from *The Ethics of War: Classic and Contemporary Readings*, ed. Gregory Reichberg, Henrik Syse and Endre Begby. (Malden, MA: Blackwell Publishing, 2006), 70.

[47] *Causa*, q. II, cans. 1, 2.

[48] *Gospel of St. Matthew* 26:52.

[49] *Causa* 23, q. IV, can. 36.

[50] *De Civitate Dei* I, 21.

[51] See Frederick Russell, *The Just War in the Middle Ages*, 76.

[52] *Causa* 23, q. III, cans. 5, 7.

[53] *Causa* 23, q. V, cans. 7, 8.

[54] *Causa* 23, q. V, can, 18.

[55] *Causa* 23, q. VI, can. 1.

[56] *Causa* 23, q. V, can. 46.

[57] *Causa* 23, q. VIII, cans. 8, 9.

[58] *Causa* 23, q. VIII, can. 28.

[59] *Summa Theologiae* II-II, Q. 40, Art. 1. All English translations are from *Summa Theologica*, trans. Fathers of the English Dominican Province (Westminster: Christian Classics, 1981).

[60] *Summa Theologiae* II-II, Q. 40, Art. 1.

[61] Cf. Frederick Russell, *The Just War in the Middle Ages*, 258. Also cf. Andrés Rosler, *Political Authority and Obligation in Aristotle* (Oxford: Oxford University Press, 2005) for a comprehensive analysis of this topic.

[62] *Summa Theologiae* II-II, Q. 40, art. 1.

[63] *Ibid.*

[64] *Ibid.*

[65] *Ibid.*

[66] Cf. Jean Porter, "The Common Good in Thomas Aquinas," In *Search of the Common Good*, ed. Patrick D. Miller and Dennis P. McCann (New York: T&T Clark International, 2005), 116-120.

[67] *Summa Theologiae* II-II, Q. 40, art. 1.

[68] *Ibid.*

[69] *Summa Theologiae* II-II, Q. 108.

[70] *Summa Theologiae* II-II, Q. 64.

[71] *Summa Theologiae* II-II, Q. 34-43.

[72] *Summa Theologiae* II-II, Q. 40, art. 1. Again, Augustine thinks that war is always sinful even when deemed necessary at times.

[73] The question persists: why does Aquinas not place the question of war for instance, alongside questions like "fraternal correction" since avenging injuries would seem kindred to this peculiar expression of charity?

[74] One may also include the notable theorists Alberico Gentili, Luis de Molina and Domingo de Soto.

[75] Cf. Hedley Bull, "The Importance of Grotius in the Study of International Relations" in *Hugo Grotius and International Relations*, ed. Hedley Bull, Benedict Kingsbury and Adam Roberts (Oxford: Clarendon Press, 1992), 73. Also cf. Albert Marrin, *War and the Christian Conscience: From Augustine to Martin Luther King, Jr.* (Chicago: Henry Regnery Company, 1971), 84 and Oliver and Joan O'Donovan (ed.) *From Irenaeus to Grotius: A Sourcebook in Christian Political Thought 100-1625* (Grand Rapids: Wm. B. Eerdman's Publishing Company, 1999), 789.

[76] Cf. Leroy Brandt Walters, Jr., *Five Classic Just-War Theories: A Study in the Thought of Thomas Aquinas, Vitoria, Suárez, Gentili and Grotius* (Ph.D. diss., Yale University, 1971), 279.

[77] It may be debatable that the modern theorists accepted the principle of right intention. In their compilation *The Ethics of War*, Reichberg, Syse and Begby conclude that this principle is "ruled out" by Vitoria and replaced by the *in bello* consideration of what types of harm are permissible to inflict (323). Seeing the great emphasis that Vitoria places on the rectitude of personal conscience with regard to both the sovereign and the lowly soldier, it is hard to conclude that right intention is so utterly expendable. Cf. Leroy Brandt Walters, Jr., *Five Classic Just-War Theories*, 322.

[78] *De jure belli* 1. The English translations is taken from John Pawley Bate in *De Indis et De Jure Belli Relectiones*, ed. Ernest Nys (New York: Oceanic Publications, 1964).

[79] Cf. *Summa Theologiae* I-II, Q. 107, art. 2, ad. 2.

[80] *De jure belli* 1.

[81] *De jure belli* 1-5.

[82] *De jure belli* 3.

[83] *De jure belli* 5. It is on the issue of property protection that Vitoria seems to give preference to positive law over natural law, arguing that even if natural law did not permit war for this reason, civil law would suffice for moral permission.

[84] Cf. Aristotle, *Politics* I, 1 and Aquinas, *Summa Theologiae* I-II, Q. 90, art. 2.

[85] *Contra Faustum* 22, 75.

[86] For Vitoria, God is the efficient cause of civil authority; the society of persons constitutes the material cause; while the prince or king constitutes a perfecting of the material cause (formal or active). Vitoria's concept of civil authority is somewhat complex and at certain points somewhat contradictory. For an

excellent and detailed analysis of this topic see Steven J. Reidy, O.P., *Civil Authority According to Francis De Vitoria* (Ph.D. Diss., *Angelicum*, Rome, 1959).

[87] *De jure belli* 13.

[88] Cf. Walters, *Five Classic Just-War Theories*, 312.

[89] *De jure belli* 14.

[90] *De jure belli* 33.

[91] *De jure belli* 60.

[92] Cf. O'Donovan, *From Irenaeus to Grotius*, 723.

[93] Cf. Bernice Hamilton, *Political Thought in Sixteenth Century Spain* (Oxford: Clarendon Press, 1963), 7.

[94] Cf. Walters, *Five Classic Just-War Theories*, 277.

[95] *De fide, spe et caritate,* Disp. XIII, 1. Since the name of this disputation is *De bello,* in the future the disputation will be cited as such. All the translations of Suárez are by Gwladys L. Williams, *Selections from Three Works of Francisco Suárez, SJ,* The Classics of International Law, no. 20, vol. 2 (Oxford: Clarendon Press, 1944) by way of *The Ethics of War: Classic and Contemporary Readings.*

[96] *De bello* I, 2.

[97] Despite his sacrosanct reputation as one of the greatest of the Scholastics, Suárez nevertheless seems to have been a man of his own time, a time of great contentiousness and sectarian hatred.

[98] *De bello* II, 1.

[99] They did not seem to agree, however, on the authority of subordinate princes to wage war. Suárez was more imperial, allowing only the supreme sovereign this authority.

[100] *De bello* II, 1.

[101] Cf. Walters, *Five Classic Just-War Theories,* 289-291.

[102] *De bello* II, 6.

[103] Suárez differs from Vitoria on the matter of whether a supreme prince can avenge injustices throughout the entire world (*De belli* IV, 3). Even though Suárez takes up this issue under the section on just cause, the way he frames his position (to the contrary) gives the impression that it is more an issue of authority and jurisdiction rather than justice.

[104] Vitoria and Suárez did, however, have a different sense of how closely connected certain precepts were with the self-evident principles of the natural law. For a thorough discussion of their views cf. Bernice Hamilton, *Political Thought in Sixteenth Century Spain*, 11-29.

[105] Cf. O'Donovan, *From Irenaeus to Grotius*, 725.

[106] Cf. O'Donovan, *From Irenaeus to Grotius*, 725.

[107] *De bello* IV, 3-4.

[108] *De bello* IV, 8.

[109] *De bello* IV, 10.

[110] *De bello* IV, 6. Cf. G.I.A.D. Draper, "Grotius' Place in the Development of Legal Ideas about War," *Hugo Grotius and International Relations*, 189.

[111] *De bello* IV, 8.

[112] Cf. O'Donovan, *From Irenaeus to Grotius,* 789.

[113] *De jure belli ac pacis* I.

[114] Some scholars contend that Grotius was unclear on the distinctions between natural and Divine law (including Evangelical law), the former often permitting things that were prohibited by the latter. Cf. Joan D. Tooke, *The Just War in Aquinas and Grotius* (London: S.P.C.K., 1965), 197. Cf. also Draper, "Grotius' Place in the Development of Legal Ideas about War," 192.

[115] Cf. *De jure belli ac pacis* I, 2, 4: "From the law of nature then which may also be called the law of nations."

[116] *De jure belli ac pacis* II, 1, 2. Translation by A.C. Campbell, *On the Law of War and Peace* (Whitefish: Kessinger Publishing, 2004). Cf. also Draper, "Grotius' Place in the Development of Legal Ideas about War," 194.

[117] It bears mentioning that this position is debatable, as some scholars thought Grotius' attempt to create a grand, international legal schema suffered under strong moralistic tendencies. For example, cf. Draper, "Grotius' Place in the Development of Legal Ideas about War," 193.

[118] *De jure belli ac pacis* II, 1, 2.

[119] *De jure belli ac pacis* I, 3, 8.

[120] Walters, *Five Classic Just-War Theories,* 313.

[121] *De jure belli ac pacis* II, 20, 40. Cf. also Walters, *Five Classic Just-War Theories,* 315.

[122] *De jure belli* II, 2, 1-5.

[123] *De jure belli* II, 2, 10.

[124] *De jure belli* II, 2, 13 and 16.

[125] *De jure belli* II, 2, 13.

[126] *De jure belli* II, 24, 7.

[127] *De jure belli ac pacis* II, 24, 9.

[128] *De jure belli ac pacis* II, 23, 6.

[129] *Catechism of the Catholic Church,* paragraph 2307 (Rome: Libreria Editrice Vaticana, 1994), citing *Gaudium et Spes,* 81, 4.

CHAPTER TWO

The First Symposium on "Just War Theory and the Wars in Afghanistan and Iraq"

Moderated by
Craig J. N. de Paulo

PROFESSOR de PAULO: I have some questions to put to the entire panel. According to Catholic just war theory, essentially founded upon the teachings of St. Augustine and St. Thomas Aquinas, and further elaborated by the magisterium, there are certain principles to which all Christian nations must adhere in order to conduct what is considered a morally justifiable war. These principles are: 1) legitimate authority, 2) just cause, 3) right intention, 4) the war must not attack innocents, but only military targets avoiding civilian populations. 5) war must be the last resort since the fifth commandment forbids the intentional destruction of human life. *The Catechism of the Catholic Church* (2309), promulgated by Pope John Paul II in 1994, also states what amounts to two additional principles: 6) that "there must be serious prospects of success" and 7) that "the use of arms must not produce evils and disorders graver than the evil to be eliminated," which is usually referred to in terms of proportionality. We should further keep in mind that the Catholic Church assumes that all war is evil since it is the result of original sin; but that in certain instances, war may be considered a necessary evil in our common desire for peace, as St. Augustine claims. Now, let us first try to apply these basic principles to the war in Afghanistan and then in Iraq.

First of all, in your opinion, can we apply these principles to the 2001 war in Afghanistan since the United States was never attacked by the nation of Afghanistan itself?

Further, as you know, the current Administration argues according to the following logic: That since Afghanistan harbored the enemy they could be justifiably considered the enemy. Do you agree with this argument and why?

I welcome anyone from the panel to address this question. Well, let me be more aggressive. Your Eminence, would you mind addressing the last question?

CARDINAL DULLES: I think it's fairly clear that it was justified since the Taliban was in charge in Afghanistan. They certainly were protecting and harboring al-Qaeda operatives and Osama bin Laden and I think we had an obligation to respond, and this would be the obvious response. I can't see why it would not be justified.

PROFESSOR de PAULO: Thank you. Colonel?

COLONEL JACOBS: Yeah, here's an interesting question for you. It's easy to have hindsight. Let's say it's before 9/11 and we have evidence which, I don't know that I would argue that it's incontrovertible or not, but we have evidence to indicate that, in fact, there is a Taliban that is supporting terrorists and there's a possibility in all likelihood that they will attack the United States. So?

PROFESSOR de PAULO: Well, let me put forth a more difficult question perhaps. That's with the 2003 war in Iraq because I would agree with His Eminence that one can argue that the war in 2001 in Afghanistan was justifiable, although I think it's also a loophole argument. With the 2003 war in Iraq there are a number of difficult questions.

First of all, do you think that the United States and its Allies exhausted all diplomatic means of resolution prior to commencing war? If someone can address that.

ARCHBISHOP O'BRIEN: I think a lot of these questions are political questions. I'm no politician and I'm no international expert, and that's why I think these questions of right and wrong, morality or immorality depends on so many political factors and situa-

tions that existed at the time that would take professionals to assess. I am not a professional in that area. I know what the Bishops
did say to the United States was that there was sufficient arguments on either side to allow a prudent person to come down either side whether the war is justified or not. There was a universal
agreement, it seems, that there were stockpiles of weapons in Iraq.
What happened to them? I don't know. The past administration
said so and the war got started and they weren't there and there
was a breakdown in intelligence.

But at the time that the decision was made, it was made in
good faith. Did they think there was an imminent possibility of
attack based on past performance of an individual who killed his
own?

Since 1992 – I was on the U.S.S. Harry S. Truman for three
days and planes would leave twenty-four hours a day to protect
the Iraqi people against their own government. That's for ten
years that's going on. So there was a cease-fire in some ways, but
the war is still continuing in Iraq and we were there to protect the
people against their own government. So you have to look at the
situation at the time the judgment was made should be good
enough, and the reasons from prudent and honest people that
come down on either side of that. One is not necessarily more
Christian than the other or more American than the other.

PROFESSOR de PAULO: Thank you. That is going to be my next
question.

With the war in Iraq, I think you will all agree, that the Allies
argued that there was "imminent threat" to our peace and the
central argument for justification of this war, then, essentially relied upon the existence of weapons of mass destruction despite
the conclusions of the delegation from the United Nations that
determined otherwise. Since weapons of mass destruction have
not ever been recovered by the Allies and the intelligence communities of the United States and Britain have since recanted this
position, was this perception sufficient justification for war?

ARCHBISHOP O'BRIEN: The perception on the part of our government was based on what they thought were facts, real evidence. And I think they made the decisions based on those facts

and if they thought we are going to be attacked, then I think the presumption is correct.

Now I can disagree with it and you can disagree with it, but they looked at all of the facts. And for one in the military or any one of us, we must have faith in our government. I think most people might say this is very confusing. We better trust this man in good faith. I hope I answered the question.

MR. MARLIN: One thing General Tommy Franks pointed out is that he had the British, Arabs, the French and the Germans who all thought there were weapons of mass destruction, so I think everyone agreed.

PROFESSOR de PAULO: You know, what I am asking is whether you think this perception was sufficient, I'll turn to Ambassador Melady, and also do you think that all diplomatic means of resolution were exhausted prior to commencing war and do you think this perception to go into Iraq was sufficient resignation?

AMBASSADOR MELADY: I felt clearly it was justified in terms of self-defense.

I think we have to lead eventually, but what can we do about preemption, who makes the decision? The leaders of the powerful nations made the proper conclusion and it was quite clear. Both Democrats and Republicans did consult with them. They had the same information he had. So certainly based on what we're discussing here the diagnosis is the perception. So what would be the guidelines for getting the information? I lived in Washington, D.C. and read this very eerie article about what one suitcase can do. We had to exit out before leaving Washington, D.C. and we all had plans to get down to the basement because it's probably reasonable to assume that being attacked in the United States would be high-profile.

The responsibility, what can we do to make it more clear that we have the responsibility of authority to what should be done? We had no questions about Afghanistan, but there are some questions about Iraq.

PROFESSOR CAPUTO: Let's go back to the discussion of preemptive strikes. We took a preemptive strike against Iraq and we were wrong. We virtually – every assumption that we made has proved to be wrong and the attacks of preemption had nothing to do or little to do with the attacks post-9/11.

We rallied the support of the international community, and we rallied all the allies against the terrorists and anti-American forces. We rallied them together in a strike which has proved to be ill-advised. We had lots of counsel from the United Nations. We have counsel from the United States Cardinals and Bishops. We had all kinds of counseling against this strike. I think in follow-up, it's costing lives, costing money, it's costing the prestige of the United States as a moral leader. Our names have been blackened in many places. Our international alliances are weakened. And we probably made the country less safe and not more safe because of the radicals against us.

With preemptive strikes you're substituting present ills for a prospective one, a possible one. You're substituting real death now for something that you may be able to prevent and you may be wrong.

It's like the argument against capital punishment. You may be wrong, and if you're wrong there's no coming back.

PROFESSOR de PAULO: Thank you.

AMBASSADOR MELADY: I won't argue necessarily for or against going into Iraq. There are a lot of things I don't like about going into Iraq.

PROFESSOR de PAULO: Well, on this point, the Allies commenced war by preemptive strike, which as you know, according to our philosophical and theological tradition on this matter, is completely contrary to the principles of the Gospel and Christian warfare.

And the question is, first of all, what are your thoughts on this problem of a preemptive strike by Christians?

And secondly, do you think the Allies were making a distinction between wars between Christian nations and wars between Christian and Muslim Nations?

PROFESSOR HAGAN: Augustine says something like the following, if I may have an opportunity to develop my thoughts, that for "the true followers of God even wars are peaceful, can you imagine, if they remove terror, greed or cruelty, for the sake of peace to restrain evildoers and to assist the good."

Now St. Thomas Aquinas would reject the notion that the Church begins with the presumption against war and he would insist that it's with the presumption that civil authority is responsible for defending the common good if a war is necessary.

PROFESSOR de PAULO: Yes, but can a preemptive strike be morally justified? That's what I am asking.

PROFESSOR HAGAN: If it satisfies those conditions, yes.

PROFESSOR de PAULO: And those conditions are that the nation is at risk?

PROFESSOR HAGAN: Exactly.

PROFESSOR de PAULO: Anyone else on the panel?

ARCHBISHOP O'BRIEN: I think the traditional just war theory has to be reviewed and be developed and in light of what Cardinal Dulles has said, we don't have legitimate government when you have terrorists. I am not saying that every preemptive strike is appropriate. Certainly we see sometimes if I know I am going to be attacked or there's a presumption that I'm going to be attacked then I have a right to take defensive action before I am attacked.

PROFESSOR de PAULO: If it's a reasonable assumption.

ARCHBISHOP O'BRIEN: If I am sure I am going to be attacked I have a right to step in. I can step in and turn the other cheek, and I probably should just as a personal thing. But I don't think we're talking about 200 million people who are willing to turn the other cheek. This is the Christian way, but there is an obligation to defend others when we are in danger of going to be harmed and harm to the innocent.

PROFESSOR de PAULO: Yes, I would agree.

PROFESSOR CAPUTO: The action taken in Iraq was not justifiably preemptive, and history has proven that to be the case. I think, it constitutes the just war theory that if you are sure that you are about to be attacked then you can certainly take preemptive action.

PROFESSOR de PAULO: When you say you are sure, there's a lot of ambiguity with that.

MR. MARLIN: I ran a government agency, one of the oldest government agencies in America. We had 400 million people annually that went through our facilities.

Everyday I would receive a list of things from the FBI, the Port Authority Police is the twentieth largest police department in the United States, about action that maybe taken, could have taken place, information of security, I saw it everyday of the week. And professionals had to make decisions on what to do. Quite frankly, prior to 9/11 on a smaller scale, preemptive measures were taken everyday of the week. Starting on September 12th I sat down with a lot of the FBI guys since September 11th, they had taken preemptive action all over this nation, okay. In parts of Queens –

PROFESSOR de PAULO: We're talking here about preemptive strikes.

MR. MARLIN: These were preemptive strikes as far as I'm concerned. They went out and their first job was to chase the enemy out of this nation. And to keep them out of this nation they did random preemptive strikes overseas, saying let it happen there, better than here.

Now, I would argue that because of all these preemptive strikes we have not had another strike during the last three years.

PROFESSOR de PAULO: I appreciate that, but what I have to point out is that, that's a practical principle, but not necessarily a Gospel one.

MR. MARLIN: You take responsibility for 400 million people and these facilities and let your mind work on that one.

PROFESSOR de PAULO: Let me repeat this question. Aside from preemptive strikes, do you think that there was a distinction made between wars between Christian nations and wars between Christian and Muslim nations?

AMBASSADOR MELADY: Let's get one thing clear. There is no tradition that says we're to be passive. The rules were you had to be a member of a church or group, and that was a matter of doctrine and so in World War II, I was a Catholic and an objector and it wasn't recognized because of a matter of Catholic teaching, so there was some varied opinions. One thing is quite clear, there is nothing in the Catholic doctrine that says you should be passive.

PROFESSOR de PAULO: With what occurred in Iraq, in your opinion, do you think there was a distinction made between Christian nations and Christian and Muslim nations with regard to the preemptive strikes in Iraq?

AMBASSADOR MELADY: I don't think there has to be a distinction for certain clear examples in the Western history of the Church, but it wasn't nations that were predominantly Christian who had attacked someone else and we would respond. We have to be careful about that and the individual acts, but certainly there is no difference in my opinion.

PROFESSOR de PAULO: My next question is with regard to the war in Iraq concerning the third principle of just war theory, and that is: In your opinion, do you think there was right intention in this war, especially since there was widespread suspicion concerning the Allies' desire for control of this oil-rich region?

AMBASSADOR MELADY: I think the suspicions are false with regard to the war in Iraq and the just war theory.

MR. MARLIN: I think the suspicions are false and meaningless. Oil crept up to $52 a barrel a couple weeks ago and if that was our design, boy, it was some dumb design. So I think that's the usual reaction that we have is that we're greedy for oil. Obviously, what happened in the past, in the aftermath of the war proves the suspicion false or the oil would be down to 30 bucks a barrel.

PROFESSOR de PAULO: Well, true or false, Mr. Marlin, I know you are a friend, however, this is what this panel is about. This suspicion was widely regarded as the *real* reason for going to war.

I'd like to know if whether you think it was the right intent of going to war in Iraq?

MR. MARLIN: There was no intent in terms of oil as far as I'm concerned. This suspicion you say has been proven false just by the fluctuation in the price of oil. It's just, you know, they were wrong.

PROFESSOR de PAULO: Okay, thank you.

AMBASSADOR MELADY: I'll avoid the temptation to answer in one sentence. Life is complicated, so the question is of major power that is to be of concern, but not to have the access to this energy supply is not the only reason, but if it were a factor, a factor as you're saying, it was the only reason, but it was a factor.

PROFESSOR CAPUTO: I think there's been shifting statements on the issue of first intent. The first intent was to stop the production of weapons of mass destruction. Then as that intent began to dissolve, then it became our opposition to a cruel dictator. But in any case, the United States, in dealing with a cruel dictator, we helped make Saddam Hussein a cruel dictator in the 80's because he was battling with Iran and we thought that was just fine. When he poisoned and gassed his own people we didn't object to that. So when did they object to his dictatorship? I mean we were silent or we even supported him. It was like in the Philippines, Kosovo, Nicaragua, Chile, so we do that all the time. So were we after oil? I don't know if we were after oil, you can't judge people's intentions, but there was this dictator and that then maybe the second reason for this action. The first reason collapsed so we then appointed ourselves, deputized ourselves in charge of making a regime change in a sovereign nation.

PROFESSOR de PAULO: Thank you. My next question I'd like to direct to Cardinal Dulles.

The most difficult question with regard to the war in Iraq surrounds the problem that the Holy See viewed this war as unjust. In fact, as you know, the pope sent Cardinal Pio Laghi to the White House to dissuade the president from attacking Iraq and, prior to this, the papal nuncio to the United Nations also delivered an official statement denouncing this war.

My question is: How can we possibly consider this war to be morally justifiable when the "Supreme Pontiff of the Universal Church" has denounced it?

CARDINAL DULLES: I think the judgment of the Supreme Pontiff on doctrinal matters is obliging on Catholics. On conventional matters, he deserves certainly a very serious hearing. I think the hearings are largely a question of credentials in terms of what he thought the difficulties would be and he knew a good deal about the Middle East, I think more than many of our foreign policy experts. I think he realized it wasn't going to be so simple to establish a democratic regime in Iraq. But I think he was trying to persuade President Bush not to intervene, and he was also trying to pressure Saddam Hussein not to make it necessary. Some people said he was trying to negotiate the resignation of Saddam Hussein in Iraq to avoid the war. So he was putting pressure on both sides. I think he made the correct judgment, which has to be taken very seriously. Obviously, he only has access to the knowledge he had, but he never said that, as far as I can remember, the

Holy Father, that the war is unjust or would trouble the conscience of the people engaged in the military or by saying it is sinful on their part.

PROFESSOR de PAULO: Well, that's another matter, another question. So you have answered the question in the sense that when the Supreme Pontiff speaks in this capacity – is it ecclesiastical arbitration?

CARDINAL DULLES: It's strictly a doctrinal statement.

ARCHBISHOP O'BRIEN: The Cardinal [Pio Cardinal Laghi] was asked the same question weeks after the conflict started and he said the pope has not proposed the position as the doctrine of the Church, but as the appeal of conscience illuminated by the faith. You neglected to mention that the Holy Father also sent the Cardinal to Saddam Hussein to negotiate, so there was some seventeen points from the United Nations that was still on the table that you haven't responded to so please show some good faith. And he had begged Saddam Hussein to do that for all these many years too. So he appealed to both sides. He made every attempt to avoid this horrible possibility.

And as His Eminence said, I think the pope probably had great insights as to the realities there and the promise of success and what it would take.

PROFESSOR de PAULO: In your opinion, was this an unjust war in Iraq?

ARCHBISHOP O'BRIEN: Once again, this is not a moral judgment that I'm making on others, and I have a free right to say what I like. It's not clear, I don't think it's actually clear enough to make an undisputed one-sided decision: It's absolutely right or it's absolutely wrong.

PROFESSOR de PAULO: Well, do you not think that the nuncio's address to the United Nations was clear about this war in Iraq.

ARCHBISHOP O'BRIEN: The nuncio's address?

PROFESSOR de PAULO: Yes.

ARCHBISHOP O'BRIEN: I have great respect for the nuncio, but he's not the pope. I don't think anyone had a right to say whether, if they had the facts, that this is immoral or taking part in this is immoral.

AMBASSADOR MELADY: In one sense it was clear that some aspects of the Holy See, the pope, had some concern. He said, bear in mind, he spent a lot of time meeting with President Bush and made the same pleadings with Saddam Hussein, but at no time do we have a statement by the Holy Father saying that this war is immoral. If you read his books and that's a great thing for us in our Roman Catholic faith. We, as Christians, will be facing this problem from time to time because our Holy Father will speak and give his position, and history has a point of view that will influence ambassadors all over the world to those right down there in Washington. And perhaps we haven't distinguished, and I've been saying this is a lesson learned as pure intentions of these matters. The point of view is that we have another agenda, an agenda of trying to prove that the Holy Father feels this way. I think probably that it's something I find disagreeable when I see someone with a very personal agenda to try to drag the pope in. He's on my side, we have him, we have him.

PROFESSOR de PAULO: Thank you. Ambassador Melady, in your opinion do you think the war in Iraq was unjust?

AMBASSADOR MELADY: What was the question?

PROFESSOR de PAULO: In your opinion, do you regard the war in Iraq as unjust?

AMBASSADOR MELADY: In my opinion, if we got involved in the war, we could be quarterbacks here, I've always felt we should take care of Saddam Hussein in some way or another. Was it a consensus with the war? We had a lot of discussion about it. The motive was right, and now that we did that, I'm clear that we should win the war with dignity and honor and proceed to other matters.

PROFESSOR de PAULO: Thank you.

PROFESSOR CAPUTO: Well, I think as Catholics we have an obligation to our own conscience. Sometimes the pope or the bishops are not right. I think they are often not right. You have to simply be bound by conscience to say that they are not right if it's indeed what you think in your heart and that you have considered very carefully what they have to say. I have been known to disagree with them. In this case, however, I happen to think they were right, and I also think they were relatively unambiguous about this war, with the war in Iraq anyway. I think they regarded the war in Afghanistan differently, as do I.

I think somewhere along the line we should go back to the discussion that Cardinal Dulles raised originally. How do you deal with a sub-national group that is not a sovereign entity? And I think that part of the answer is that you don't wage war on a nation. I think some of the most effective things that were done to keep the nation safe since 9/11 had been police action, in Spain, Germany, Saudi Arabia and various places where we have been able to apprehend by the cooperation of the International Police Community to apprehend anyone before they were about to cause trouble and located cells. I don't think waging a war on another sovereign nation is necessarily the best way to deal with this. I think in the case of Iraq it was proven to be a bad one. And I am not one to play Monday morning quarterback. I was against this from the get-go. I was against this the Saturday before it started.

PROFESSOR de PAULO: Thank you. Another question, what seems to be an important personal one, which I'll direct to Archbishop O'Brien.

Excellency, do you not see it as a conceivable moral problem for Catholic soldiers fighting in this war since if they have "formed consciences" it would appear that if they felt that this was an unjust war, and therefore, they would have to violate the known position of the Holy See to do their job and what we may assume is the will of the Holy Father? Can you comment on that?

ARCHBISHOP O'BRIEN: Well, I think the question is: did they violate their conscience? And if an individual volunteers to serve in the armed forces he must have some kind of belief that the war is justified.

If in a particular war he has some doubts, he has every right and option to say to his commanders, this is how I feel about it and therefore, I can't go along with it. If he thinks, if he's convinced that this is an immoral war or that actions within that war are immoral, that individual has an obligation, an obligation not to, if we are convinced that the individual thinks this is a wrong war.

When I was a captain back in Vietnam, we had the draft and some that were brought into the military didn't like war at all and as the chaplain, I very often had to go to bat for soldiers and plead their cause and say that this man should not have to take up arms. I think chaplains would do that today when an individual comes to see them. When someone comes to a chaplain, and says I am totally opposed to this war, I think it's out and out immoral, the chaplain would then go to bat for that soldier as best he could to try and present his cause.

PROFESSOR de PAULO: I mean if I were a soldier or officer, even though I made an oath to the Constitution to take orders from my superiors; but, as a Roman Catholic, in good conscience, I know that the pope is, after all, the Vicar of Jesus Christ.

ARCHBISHOP O'BRIEN: Well, I am Catholic too. I have no less regard for the pope.

PROFESSOR de PAULO: But if I were a soldier it would be impossible for me to violate my conscience to go to war.

In this instance, do you see this as a conceivable problem having experienced that in your capacity as chaplain?

ARCHBISHOP O'BRIEN: Well, I think if I were convinced that this individual is justified in his sincerity, is sincerely opposed to this war for whatever reason, if he thinks it would be a sin if he took part in this war, as chaplain, I would try to do the best I can to bring to bat that man's issues and either have him go to another unit or do some other kind of public work.

PROFESSOR de PAULO: All right. Thank you. There is a question from the audience and also a question from Dr. John Haas.

There are many that believe that the president used these wars as a Holy war or crusade, and the individual wants to know what the panel thinks about this.

PROFESSOR HAGAN: I think that's nonsense.

COLONEL JACOBS: I also believe it's nonsense. Here's something to think about. There's an underlying strategic condition that the administration has that you can either agree with or disagree with. There are only two democracies in the Southwest edge, one is Israel and one is Turkey. All Arab countries, nations, states, and so on. Keep in mind they didn't abide by any Catholic doctrine. There are no Arab states that are democracies. A point of this Administration is that if we would merely inoculate the region with democracy that it would spread and then ultimately the entire region would be democratic Muslim. And ultimately, the entire region, not only would the people we save, they wouldn't have to live under these deplorable conditions, but also the entire Western world would be safer. That's particularly significant in an era with nuclear weapons and certainly nuclear materials that are relatively easy to manufacture. I'm not saying one should agree or disagree with it, but certainly that's the view of some people in the Administration and certainly a factor for the decision that drove us into Iraq.

PROFESSOR de PAULO: Thank you. Professor Caputo.

PROFESSOR CAPUTO: I don't think he (the President) is imprudent enough to say that it's a holy war. But I think he plays that card implicitly, his rhetoric, his appeal to the Christian Right is implicitly allowing people to think that that's what it is, but I don't think he's imprudent enough to say that's what it is. But I think that goes to his certain mind without saying.

AMBASSADOR MELADY: Well, I don't think there's any concrete evidence that the president, first of all, is on any kind of crusade or anything like that. He's very clear about the benefit of establishing another form of government along the lines of democracy in Iraq and that is clear. I think if you talk to people on both sides of the fence on that, that's clear.

PROFESSOR de PAULO: There is a question from Dr. John M. Haas, John Cardinal Krol Chair Emeritus of Moral Theology at St. Charles Borromeo Seminary in Philadelphia, who is currently the President of the National Catholic Bio-Ethics Center, also here in Philadelphia.

DR. HAAS: Thank you, Professor de Paulo. A lot of discussion has been given to justifiability of war, the justifiability of preemptive strike. So my question is: Can this war be justified if it is looked upon as the concluding phase of the original Iraq War, which few people judge to be unjustified?

In other words, we would not even need a preemptive strike if they were seen as the conclusion of the war that began by George Bush the First?

ARCHBISHOP O'BRIEN: I think that's very plausible. I don't think the war ever really ended in that cease-fire. We were still defending the Iraqi people only in different ways then. The cease-fire was never settled into a formal peace agreement and so I would agree very strongly with that.

PROFESSOR de PAULO: Thank you. There is one other question from Professor Daniel Tompkins, my boss, and Director of the Intellectual Heritage Program at Temple University.

PROFESSOR TOMPKINS: The war in Iraq, I am trying to get away a little bit from the particulars of the war in Iraq, so the war in Iraq was presented to us in part as a war of humanitarian interest on behalf of the Shiite population and humanitarian grounds were also used to justify the war in Afghanistan. On the very same grounds it was used to justify NATO, American action in Bosnia and Kosovo. So it's one long string of wars that called themselves humanitarian. Humanitarian appeals to all of us, but what I'm really interested to learn today from the expert panel is how humanitarian intervention fits into five principles and the two possibilities that Professor de Paulo listed for justifying the war. Is intervention of this sort traditionally covered by the principle of just cause?

CARDINAL DULLES: It seems to me that it does fit into the just war principles as I understand them, and I think it certainly has a right intention and just cause and could be legitimate authority to wage humanitarian intervention. I think it could. Now of course there's a question of prudence and a question of proportionality and all discrimination and all of those other questions have come up, but I think in general we cannot condemn humanitarian intervention as being conquered for the just war doctrine.

AMBASSADOR MELADY: We've seen examples where the Holy Father himself has called for the use of military. In fact, he called me in regard to Somalia. We didn't have much of an embassy there, but we did have concrete evidence and foundation and so forth and so he asked me to ask the president, which I did, and the president authorized the use of the military to open up the harbors and roads to get the food in and medical supplies. The same thing happened with Liberia and I was called in when the Liberian Government had collapsed. The people were being killed. They sent troops in. In a more general way to stop the suffering that was going on. In that case the president put military warships around the coast, which helped to tranquilize...so there was the use of military for humanitarian purposes.

PROFESSOR CAPUTO: I think that if all of the conditions were met you could have a humanitarian intervention. I think one of the sticking wounds would be in this case proper authority. One nation can't deputize itself to affect a regime change in another sovereign nation just because it doesn't like what's going on there. So in this case you'd have to have a broad international concession that is was a need for international human need and recognized the gross negligence and required intervention.

PROFESSOR de PAULO: And one final question. After everything we've talked about, do you think that these principles still apply to contemporary warfare and the problem of terrorism? If so, why?

CARDINAL DULLES: I think the major principles, the five you've enumerated, plus the two additions of your own that you stated in your introductory statement, do certainly apply and do apply always and everywhere with all forms of warfare. I think there are a lot of secondary principles that have come into the tradition which are contingent upon several types of warfare and they change between conventional warfare and perhaps professional military moving towards modern national total war and then nuclear war and terrorist war. There are a lot of changes that we have to reckon with, so I think that terrorism does present us with a whole new set of problems that are not really adequately dealt with by the standard of just war theory. There's lots of room for creativity in applying those general principles of just war to this kind of a situation of terrorism. This is not a question of war between sovereign states. It's a faction against a whole civilization.

PROFESSOR de PAULO: Thank you. Mr. Marlin?

MR. MARLIN: I have one line that Henry Kissinger wrote: "Never before has it been necessary to conduct a war with neither front lines nor geographic definition and, at the same time, to rebuild fundamental principles of world order to replace the traditional ones," which went up in the smoke of the World Trade Center and the Pentagon.

The rules have changed, as we have never seen before. They brought a bomb into New York City and George Bush, on September 13th, found his voice when he went down to Ground Zero. And unless you spend some time down there, unless you knew, in my case I knew those buildings well, but more importantly, I came from a part of Queens where every Catholic parish within the neighborhood averaged twenty-four dead in that parish. And if you live in New York or you are a New Yorker and you went through that, we in New York have a very different view of the world today because it struck us so close. The rules have changed. The times have changed and these principles we establish still apply, but we have to recognize that it's just so different. And if you have ever been down to Ground Zero, you'll look and see how different it is with the threats we face and that means our rules have to change which brings us back to the preemptive issues I was dealing with earlier. We have an obligation by judgment of moral obligations to use every preventive measure we can take hold of to make sure that does not happen again. Thank you.

PROFESSOR de PAULO: Thank you all very much, and most especially our distinguished panelists for their kind and thoughtful participation in this event. Have a wonderful evening and thank you very much.

SUPPLEMENTAL STATEMENTS

Although all of the panelists from the symposium were invited to contribute supplemental statements in order to further clarify their assumptions, arguments and positions, Avery Cardinal Dulles, S.J. was the only panelist to reply to our request.

STATEMENT FROM AVERY CARDINAL DULLES, S.J.

There can be no question of abandoning just war principles. They are basic rules of morality. War by its very nature causes harm to persons and property. The infliction of harm has to be justified. If the issues can be settled by negotiation or arbitration without recourse to arms, this should be done. For a war to be justified, there must be a right intention, a just cause, and a reasonable prospect of success without infliction of disproportionate damage. Because war is a conflict between states or coalitions, it must be waged under a legitimate authority that can command corporate actions. Harm to innocent third parties should be avoided to the extent possible.

The rules of just war theory, as contrasted with the principles, change according to the evolving methods of warfare. In modern times, just war theorists have usually presumed that wars are waged between sovereign states that are contending for disputed territory. Before fighting actually begins, notice is given, usually by a formal declaration of war. The defending state would have time to prepare a defense before its capacity to respond would be destroyed. According to the rules, the fighting is done by soldiers dressed in uniforms, who openly display their weapons. War, so conceived, can be terminated by the surrender of the government of a belligerent state. Once the surrender has been given, the people of the nation must acknowledge defeat and lay down their arms.

When these conditions are verified, just war theory can provide a set of rather specific rules: for example, that one should declare a war before beginning one; that aggressive wars are forbidden; that pre-emptive strikes are illicit unless an attack is imminent; that civilians should not be targeted; and that prisoners of war should be accorded rights enshrined in certain conventions.

Many of these rules were already cast into doubt by modern total warfare, which involves not just armies, but the entire citizenship of the belligerent nation. Further problems were raised by modern nuclear warfare, which can destroy a nation's ability to respond in a matter of seconds. The emergence of international terrorism in recent decades has made it still more difficult to apply some of the conventional rules. When terrorists attack, the belligerent is no longer a nation-state with an identifiable army but a more or less invisible faction of persons who can strike without notice and inflict untold damage. The objective of the aggressor is not to gain more territory but to wreak harm and confusion, perhaps to annihilate the very fabric of society.

The proper response to terrorism can scarcely be negotiation, because there is no authority with whom to negotiate and because even if agreement with a prominent leader could be achieved, there would be no way of bringing his followers to observe the terms of the agreement. To wait passively for the terrorists to attack first would be fatal because they would have the capacity to repeat acts similar to those of September 11, 2001.

It seems to me that any sound plan of action has to aim at the political reconfiguration of that part of the world where terrorism is being bred and from which the terrorist attacks have been coming. If we could do so with a broad coalition of free-world republics, that should be done, but if other free countries do not take a realistic view of the situation, the United States may have to move ahead as part of a smaller alliance. Inaction or futile attempts at negotiation would both mean guaranteed failure.

CARDINAL DULLES' RESPONSES TO THE INITIAL QUESTIONS PUT TO THE PANELISTS

To Qu. 1. Afghanistan was under the rule of Taliban, which was closely identified with terrorism and was shielding Osama bin Laden, who had unquestionably attacked the United States. For this reason I believe that our attack on Afghanistan was legitimate.

To Qu. 2. We had been negotiating with Saddam Hussein for ten years after he had violated the terms of the peace of 1991. The UN had unsuccessfully tried to deal with Saddam Hussein by diplomatic means, but did not have the collective will to proceed to the next obvious step. Further negotiation would only have put Saddam Hussein in a stronger position than before. Thus we had come to the point of last resort.

To Qu. 3. "Imminent threat" is not one of the seven principles of just war on the list distributed for this conference. With what we now think we know, it appears that Saddam Hussein did not in fact pose an imminent threat to the United States, though at the time it appeared probable that he did pose such a threat.

As for weapons of mass destruction, Saddam Hussein was unwilling to demonstrate that he did not have them, though he had ample opportunity to do. And so it could legitimately be pre-sumed that he did have them. If in fact he did not (as now seems to be the case), he certainly was aiming to acquire them, as well as biological and chemical weapons, which had been part of his ar-senal in the recent past.

To Qu. 4. There is no general prohibition of pre-emptive strikes in the seven principles listed above. If the enemy has the will and the capacity to strike without warning, it may be fatal to wait for him to attack before we respond.

It is a mistake to suppose that the allies were singling out Muslim nations as enemies. A number of Muslim states were among the allies. Generally speaking, Americans feel no hostility to Islam as such; they assume that the majority of Muslims are de-cent and peace-loving, even though some passages of the Koran appear to countenance violence against non-Muslims. The aim of the war was only to prevent the type of rogue behavior displayed by Al Quaeda.

To Qu. 5. To the best of my knowledge, the war was not about oil. It is about irresponsible governments that breed terrorism and threaten to bring down civilization.

To Qu. 6. The Pope and the Holy See probably have better knowl-edge of the Middle East than most American experts. I suspect that they felt that the war had insufficient prospect of success un-less the Allies were to inflict disproportionate damage, making a desert out of Iraq. But this was a prudential estimate, not a mag-isterial teaching that the faithful were bound to believe. Following the same just war principles, the Bush administration arrived at a different prudential judgment.

To Qu. 7. According to the *Catechism of the Catholic Church* "the evaluation of these conditions for moral legitimacy belongs to the prudential judgment of those who have responsibility for the common good," i.e. the civil government (CCC 2309). If each indi-vidual had to reach a personal judgment, it would be impossible for the nation to act effectively even when war was just, because many of the citizens would not be able to verify the reasons for themselves. Besides, it would be excessive to burden the con-sciences of private persons with the duty to evaluate matters on which full information is available only to a few experts. In extreme cases, of course, the injustice of a war may be evident to all persons of good will. If particular individuals are convinced that a given war is unjust, they should not be required to fight. They may be assigned to some kind of alternative service.

To Qu. 8. The seven principles do still apply, but the application is different than in conventional wars of the pre-nuclear and pre-terrorist era. A new set of rules or secondary principles needs to be generated to respond to current conditions.

One should not expect too much from the principles. They do not unequivocally tell us whether a given war is just or not. It is always necessary to ascertain the facts and then to make a prudent judgment as to whether the conditions for a just war obtain. Without accurate information and good judgment, the principles could be abused to support an unjust war or to forbid a just one.

CHAPTER THREE

The Second Symposium on "Just War Theory, the 2003 War in Iraq and the Significance of the Papacy"

Moderated by
Craig J. N. de Paulo and Patrick A. Messina

P ROFESSOR de PAULO: Ladies and gentlemen, I want to thank you all for coming this evening, especially my students; I am very grateful. I'm Craig de Paulo and this is a symposium on "Just War Theory, the 2003 War in Iraq and the Significance of the Papacy." This event, I should tell you, is following a previous Symposium that I organized right here at the Union League of Philadelphia almost two years ago that had about five hundred people in attendance from all over the country. On that panel, we had the renowned theologian, Avery Cardinal Dulles, Archbishop Edwin O'Brien, Conservative political columnist George Marlin, professor and philosopher, John D. Caputo, Dr. Joseph Hagan, Ambassador Thomas Melady and others...largely policy makers on that panel, except for Cardinal Dulles and Professor Caputo, and we may have neglected a few important philosophical details. That is the purpose of tonight's Symposium. So, we are going to try to pursue a few more sophisticated points that may result in a more comprehensive discussion. And the first session that I will be moderating is going to concentrate mostly on the relation of the

Holy See to the 2003 war in Iraq and the idea of conscience. The second session will be moderated by my colleague, Professor Patrick Messina, who will be once again taking up the question of the traditional criteria of just war theory and attempting to apply them to the 2003 Iraq War. So let me begin by introducing my friend, the President of the Union League of Philadelphia, Mr. Frank Giordano.

(Applause)

MR. GIORDANO: It is my pleasure to welcome you here this evening on behalf of our Board of Directors and the entire membership of the Union League. For the past one hundred and forty four years, the League has provided a forum for thought provoking discussions as you are going to have here this evening. The League started out in support of Abraham Lincoln and the Union cause, most importantly the abolition of slavery, and over all those years – through the past one hundred and forty four – it has been the center of many events in our history. But it is interesting...I don't think we have ever had an event that discussed the Papacy and just war. But, it is great to have you here this evening, so I hope that you enjoy yourselves. Thank you.

PROFESSOR de PAULO: Thank you very much. Let me also very briefly introduce our panelists now. First, to my left is Professor Frederick Van Fleteren, actually, a former mentor of mine, a world renowned scholar in Augustine and the author and editor of many volumes on Augustine and the Augustinian tradition...Professor Van Fleteren is from La Salle University.

Let me also introduce Professor Brian Kane, who is the Chair of the Department of Philosophy and Theology at De Sales University, a new friend of mine who wrote his doctorate and, subsequently, a book on just war theory and the role of the papacy. Thank you for joining us.

We welcome Professor Joseph Margolis of the Philosophy Department at Temple University, a very renowned philosopher, with far too many books and articles for me ever to mention at this occasion. Thank you for joining us.

And of course, I would like to welcome my boss; I have to invite him to everything I do under the threat of excommunication...Dr. Daniel Tompkins, who is Professor of Classics and the

Director of the Intellectual Heritage Program at Temple University. Thank you so much for joining us. And, of course, Professor Messina whom I have already introduced.

I decided to have us sit around a table this evening. The previous symposium was done very formally. There was a dais table, and I was at a lectern, and my position there was, let us say, contentiously polite. But, as I said, it mostly resulted in a focus on policy issues regarding the 2001 War in Afghanistan and the 2003 war in Iraq.

So, this evening, let's have more of a conversation. And I'd say the first session that I will be conducting, I want to concentrate on the role of the Holy See, mostly because this was a question that was not sufficiently treated in the previous symposium.

One of the most difficult questions in my estimation with the 2003 War in Iraq surrounds the problem that the Holy See viewed this war as unjust. In fact, as you may recall, His late Holiness, Pope John Paul II, sent Cardinal Pio Laghi to the White House to dissuade the President from attacking Iraq...and prior to this, the Papal Nuncio to the United Nations, who also delivered an official statement denouncing this war. So, my questions during this session will focus on the significance of the Holy See.

First of all, and I would like to begin, if I may, with Professor Kane. How significant do you think was the role of the Holy See, and specifically, the involvement of Pope John Paul II in what amounted to an international moral debate surrounding the 2003 War in Iraq?.

PROFESSOR KANE: I think the papal role was very significant in terms of mediating the discussion even to the extent, I think, of the Bush Administration sending emissaries to the Vatican in order to try to have the pope moderate his stance upon the War in Iraq. I think, finally, the end-decision of the Bush Administration was that Pope John Paul II would not change his mind, and therefore, the discussion ended and the Bush Administration decided to pursue the war for its own purposes. But certainly, prior to the command to begin military action, there was an ongoing dialogue between the Holy See and the Bush Administration regarding the legitimacy of the war in Iraq, preemptively.

PROFESSOR VAN FLETEREN: Are we supposed to say something?

PROFESSOR de PAULO: Sure, you may, Professor Van Fleteren.

PROFESSOR VAN FLETEREN: When the present pope was Head of the Congregation of the Faith,[1] he sent a letter concerning the last election. He sent it to, I think, the clergy in this country, the bishops and so forth. And in that statement he said that one could disagree with the pope about the morality of this war and remain within the veil of Catholicism.

So I am not exactly sure...I think that it is an overstatement to say that the papacy has condemned this war. I think that would be my first point. Maybe we can leave it there.

The second thing I would ask is if there is a condemnation, what kind of theological note that you would place on that? Does it say that it is the pope's personal magisterium, or is it the Church's magisterium...is it? So you need to define something. So, in other words, I think it is a bit too simplistic, in my opinion, to say that there is one Vatican opinion on this war that we all have to kind of hope that we...I suppose that will be controversial enough to get...

PROFESSOR KANE: I would agree with that. I don't think that the pope is speaking – in terms of the statements on the war – I do not think the intent of the those statements was to define magisterially the one position. I would, however, say that it's clear that the position that the pope articulated has resonance within the papal tradition.

PROFESSOR de PAULO: If I may insert this, I wasn't saying this earlier, Professor Van Fleteren, about the papacy as such, but about the Holy See...that official statements from the Holy See – that is in the diplomatic capacity of the pope through the nuncio and through his emissary – said that the war was unjust.

PROFESSOR VAN FLETEREN: I have not seen those statements. I know that he has said...is it before the war? He said the people that are doing this have a grave responsibility. And he said something along that line, and I think that that's something we'd all agree with...right? But I don't, in that statement and in other statements, think that there is one position on the war, that is, one

Catholic position on the war. That's my opinion, and that's up for discussion.

PROFESSOR de PAULO: You do raise another question. Professor Van Fleteren said there's not necessarily one Vatican position on the war. So let me ask this question: which position is the position of the Vatican, and which is higher, the position of the Prefect for the Congregation of the Faith, then Cardinal Ratzinger, or the Apostolic Nuncio – the pope's ambassador? In your estimation, Professor Kane, which do you think is the higher position that's representing the Vatican position?

PROFESSOR KANE: I would find it difficult to gauge, you know, a hierarchical position between those two men. It seems to me that they're both, in some ways, articulating views of the papacy, but they're different functions. And so I don't think that you can necessarily expect, you know, to equate, at least, an ambassador's position with the Prefect of the Congregation of the Faith.

PROFESSOR de PAULO: Okay. Professor Margolis?

PROFESSOR MARGOLIS: I would like to draw attention to another dimension of the question, which you ask. I mean, those of us who are privy to the Vatican range of possibilities, so to say with regard to authoritative statements, this problem has a kind of intramural aspect which is difficult. I mean that I was struck by the following consideration that the question in the United States and in the Western world with collecting support or focusing criticism on, let us say, Bush's policies and commitments are an issue of power, which has obvious importance in effective international politics.

But there are two things that strike me about all of this, that is that the question of the moral authority, let us say on the just war issue in terms of the papacy, is problematic at the present time in a number of ways, not the least of which is, of course, the fact that there are, at least, two world class religions coming from, more or less, the same sources in a way that are diametrically opposed within a range of positions that are also problematic; in the Muslim world, it is extremely problematic to decide what could be counted on as reasonably authoritative.

The divisions in the Muslim world are easily matched in the West...in the Catholic world and also in the secular and in the endlessly many different sub-worlds within the Western world. And that there seems to be no prospect...I am convinced that there is no prospect in terms of the realities around the world of a convergence of views.

PROFESSOR VAN FLETEREN: Concerning the war?

PROFESSOR MARGOLIS: Concerning the definition of just war or of terrorism or any of the essentially contested notions that are being considered. And that, therefore, this colors, in my opinion, the whole way of casting the question; it can be answered in a certain way, but I have a feeling that we are running the risk of returning to this problem in an idiom, which is precisely the sight for the kind of contests that we are now facing. It seems to me that we have to break out of that – that is my honest opinion – regardless of personal convictions and convictions within acceptably authoritative sources of moral conviction and authority and so... There is no authority that is being recognized, let us say, jointly by Christianity and Islam. I think that that is clear.

PROFESSOR KANE: Well, I would add, I think that the papacy, in a sense, does have a special role in international politics precisely because, in some ways, it serves as the only institution which can, in fact, involve itself in those kinds of discussions. I agree that the conversation internationally is fragmented, and its is very difficult to have any sort of consensus on, you know, what legitimate authority means, especially in light of terrorism, for example, and so yes, the United Nations certainly has not fulfilled that same kind of goal.

PROFESSOR MARGOLIS: No...well, I think we are in a chaotic and dangerous state right now and that we need to recognize that, but if I can just put in a slightly different edge to the question. Ultimately, there is a serious problem that I think we all recognize about the way in which what are loosely called arguments deriving from reason or arguments deriving from faith can even be brought together commensurably for purposes of debating what would be an acceptable way of proceeding.

Now, that seems to me to color the entire question of the just war concept or of the proper interpretation of terrorism, and I would just like to emphasize that – and I will shut up after that point – that without that background, I have the feeling that we threaten ourselves with being snookered innocently into a way of handling the problem which fails us at a moment when we dare not fail, if I may put it that way.

PROFESSOR de PAULO: Let me ask you then – and Professor Kane was heading in this direction – so you do not think that the pope has a unique moral authority?

PROFESSOR MARGOLIS: I do not, to be honest.

PROFESSOR de PAULO: Okay…in as much as he is a head of state and that he is able to engage in discussion with other heads of state in that capacity?

PROFESSOR MARGOLIS: I think he has a unique role to play, but I do not think that that entails a unique position respecting moral authority.

PROFESSOR de PAULO: You do not think so theoretically or you do not think so practically? Because practically would seem to me that he has a real role.

PROFESSOR MARGOLIS: I do not deny that. If you put it in terms of, let us say, the reception of his statements, there is no question that he carries enormous authority. I would say political authority presented in a moral idiom, okay?

PROFESSOR de PAULO: Right.

PROFESSOR MARGOLIS: But that leaves still the deeper question about the possibilities of demonstrating the validity of moral or moral political positions. And there, I hope you will not mind if I am entirely candid?

PROFESSOR de PAULO: Not at all.

PROFESSOR MARGOLIS: I think there is no possibility of discovering in some cognitive way what the right normalcy rules are, though there are perfectly reasonable views about how human beings should behave, I agree to that.

Now, it seems to me that the history of this question has led us to a point where not only is this a problem, but also there are competing authorities at every conceivable level who are saying, well, there is an authority, but we have it and you don't; and the other side, let us say, will say, no, we have it and you don't.

It seems to me that it is impossible to go this way now – that is my feeling – that that is the source of creating insoluble problems that we are deepening rather than ameliorating.

PROFESSOR de PAULO: Thank you…someone else? Professor Van Fleteren?

PROFESSOR VAN FLETEREN: It seems to me that the just war theory…I would agree with a lot of what you said, but it seems to me that the just war theory has been a rational attempt to come to grips with what is essentially irrational situations. And I would think that that is what we should be doing, that is to try with our reason to come to grips with these moral problems.

PROFESSOR MARGOLIS: Yes.

PROFESSOR VAN FLETEREN: And I do think that – like for example, let's take a different thing, but the problem will show. I think it was a very good thing that the Vatican came out and said in that document that there are things more important than merely sovereignty.

I think that was a very good statement, and that is being argued today precisely in Iraq and so forth, but I think it is a good thing for some moral authority – whether everyone agrees with them or not, or everyone recognizes that authority – to come out with a statement like that. So I do not know if you agree with that or disagree with that, even though there may be some people that do not recognize his authority. It is still a good thing to have a moral authority come out and say something like that.

PROFESSOR MARGOLIS: Well, I find myself in a kind of awkward spot because I agree with the pope's condemnation of the American invasion of Iraq; I agree with that.

PROFESSOR VAN FLETEREN: And you understand my point is that I am not sure he has condemned it himself. Condemned is too strong maybe.

PROFESSOR MARGOLIS: I mean, he may have made a number of statements which need to be reconciled with one another, and, at one point, he does condemn it and, at other points, he puts it in another way.

PROFESSOR de PAULO: Let me return to that point for a moment. These diplomatic statements that were given in the name of the pope as the sovereign by way of the Apostolic Nuncio and his envoy, how directly, in your opinion, do you think these statements represent the pope's personal view?

PROFESSOR VAN FLETEREN: Are you talking to me?

PROFESSOR de PAULO: All of you.

PROFFESSOR KANE: My sense is I think that they do accurately reflect his view of the war.

PROFESSOR VAN FLETEREN: Okay. And you think it is his personal view…that was the question.

PROFESSOR KANE: Yes, I think it is also his personal view.

PROFESSOR VAN FLETEREN: Also, you mean it is not just…

PROFESSOR KANE: Both, yes; both diplomatic and personal.

PROFESSOR VAN FLETEREN: But is it a theological position or a philosophical position?

PROFESSOR KANE: Yes, I think it is a theological position as well.

PROFESSOR VAN FLETEREN: One that Catholics must hold or…

PROFESSOR KANE: I do not think that he was…again, in his role as head of the Church, I do not think that those statements were meant to be definitive statements of the faith.

PROFESSOR de PAULO: This is what I want to pursue; how directly…if they represent the pope's view, how equivocal then? Professor Van Fleteren is saying that the Vatican view is equivocal; this is something I would like to pursue for the moment.

PROFESSOR VAN FLETEREN: I am not saying that. I am saying that you do not have to hold that position to be a Catholic.

PROFESSOR de PAULO: With all due respect, we have not arrived at that question. That is one I definitely want to pursue with you, but the first view is that . . .

PROFFESSOR VAN FLETEREN: There's no one Catholic view.

PROFESSOR de PAULO: That is your position.

PROFESSOR VAN FLETEREN: No one Catholic view.

PROFESSOR de PAULO: Okay. The view that I want to pursue, as moderator of the first session, is how closely do the statements made by the nuncio and his emissary represent the pope's view? In Professor Kane's opinion, they represent them directly and it is also, you think, in your opinion, personal. Professor Van Fleteren, what is your view on that?

PROFESSOR MARGOLIS: I would add…

PROFESSOR VAN FLETEREN: I do not want this to become a battle on authority, but that is not the way it was presented to begin with.

PROFESSOR de PAULO: Well, this is an important point for further questions that I have to pursue with you.

PROFESSOR MARGOLIS: Could one say that there may well be valid Catholic views on this which are incompatible with one another?

PROFESSOR de PAULO: In your opinion, sure.

PROFESSOR MARGOLIS: Do my opinions . . .

PROFESSOR de PAULO: That is not the question I am pursuing at the moment, but, yes.

PROFFESSOR MARGOLIS: Within an informed Catholic world, is it possible? I have heard Catholics at different levels of authority say Bush was entirely justified in what he did, and others who said this is an evil move. Okay?

PROFESSOR KANE: I think the answer to that question is clearly yes, so that there is a diversity of views within the Catholic community on the justification of the war.

PROFESSOR MARGOLIS: Was it valid in some sense?

PROFESSOR KANE: Yes, because it has not been formally defined as being definitively held. I mean, prior to the war, Michael Novak[2] traveled to the Vatican to try to convince John Paul II of the view of the Bush Administration that the use of force was, actually, a continuation of the use of force in Iraq.

PROFESSOR de PAULO: However, Professor Kane, can there be many Catholic views?

PROFESSOR KANE: Yes.

PROFESSOR de PAULO: As there are as many Catholics; is this part of what you are saying?

PROFESSOR KANE: I would not go that far.

PROFESSOR de PAULO: Surely you will agree that there is an official Catholic position? Is there one official Catholic position? Is there an official Catholic position for the Conference of Catholic Bishops in the United States? Is there an official position for the Vatican, an official position for the Episcopal Conference in Italy and elsewhere? Can we say there is a multiplicity of official positions?

PROFESSOR KANE: There is an official position, I would say, on the statement of principles, namely, the use of certain principles to analyze the situation. But as far as what you do with those principles and how you apply them, there is, I would say, a certain amount of diversity of opinions.

PROFESSOR VAN FLETEREN: Would you also include the Bishops of Iraq, for example, and the Bishops of Iraq that seem to justify it. I think if you are going to take these other statements, you would have to take these too. And it comes to my point: I do not think there is one Catholic position on this war. I think we can discuss this question, in other words, regardless of the question of authority.

PROFESSOR MARGOLIS: Could I press two more versions?

PROFESSOR de PAULO: Maybe in one moment. But I must say, my objectives are very clear. I only have until seven o'clock, and I said that I would give you a break, and I have to pursue because my publisher says so. (laughter)

PROFESSOR VAN FLETEREN: Publisher's minds can be changed, as you know. (more laughter)

PROFESSOR de PAULO: What I am interested in here, is whether there is one Catholic view higher than another? I am a professor of philosophy; my degree is in the name of the pope, as a matter of fact. I am a pontifical doctor; does this mean that my view is as authoritative as, for instance, the Archbishop of Philadelphia, who is, in his capacity, a successor of the Apostles? And in his capacity as a cardinal, he is also a direct representative of the pope. Is my view equivalent or higher or inferior to a view by the Conference of Bishops, or is the view by the Vatican? Let me be more specific: is the Nuncio or the Secretary of State higher? Is there one view higher than another in any of your opinions?

PROFESSOR VAN FLETEREN: Well, you want to say something? (gesturing to Professor Kane).

PROFESSOR KANE: You have the floor first.

PROFESSOR VAN FLETEREN: Well, the Nuncio is . . . but he is the representative of the Vatican as a political state, right? To America, he is the ambassador. As the ambassador, I think his statements are good to listen to. I would listen to them, but I listen to a lot of ambassadors, right?

PROFESSOR de PAULO: Well, ambassadors represent the official view of the head of state, so if I want to get the official view of the president of the United States, for instance, in his discussion . . .

PROFESSOR VAN FLETEREN: It is a political statement.

PROFESSOR de PAULO: (Continuing his thought above) In his [president's] discussion with another nation, I am going to look to his ambassador, is this not true?

PROFESSOR VAN FLETEREN: I do not think that it is a theological statement.

PROFESSOR de PAULO: Well, slowly, these are fine points that I do not want to skip over. So, in your view, there is no Catholic view higher than another whether it is sovereign, diplomatic or otherwise?

PROFESSOR VAN FLETEREN: On the Iraq war?

PROFESSOR de PAULO: The Iraq war is what we are discussing, absolutely, fine. On the Iraq war, there is no . . .

PROFESSOR VAN FLETEREN: I would say there is no Catholic authoritative statement. And I am going to say that again. I can't do anything but repeat it. There's not one Catholic view . . .

PROFESSOR de PAULO: The record has it. Let me ask you. . .

PROFESSOR KANE: I would like to add, but it is a paradoxical answer, which is, I think, that the pope has greater moral authority in terms of defining the doctrines of the Church, but that moral authority is always seen in the context of the Tradition, which is historical and long term. And so when we are looking at the application of principles to particular historical circumstances, there is more latitude in terms of the definitive positions of individual Catholics, although, within that discussion, it is clearly true that the pope has a greater weight to give to the answer.

PROFESSOR VAN FLETEREN: Than I do.

PROFESSOR de PAULO: Professor Tompkins?

PROFESSOR TOMPKINS: I want to suggest "the dog that did not bark" theory, you know, the crime was solved because the dog did not bark, and therefore, it knew its owner. The dog that did not bark in this case seems to me the pope's disinclination on this issue to speak "*ex cathedra*."[3] If he had spoken *ex cathedra*, that would have settled this argument. He did not, and he knew...I mean, you got to be smart to be pope, and he knew that by not speaking *ex cathedra*, he was opening up a terrain for discussion, which we are witnessing.

PROFESSOR de PAULO: This is an interesting point.

PROFESSOR KANE: Let me add one other piece to that, which is that within the context of the development of papal thought, out of all of the popes in the twentieth century, John Paul II is the only one who has made definitive statements on the morality of any wars. He made one comment on the fiftieth anniversary of World War II, and then the Iraq war was also a very clear statement with regard to his analysis of the morality of the particular war. If you look at the rest of the popes in the twentieth century, they do not even come close to the specificity of the statements that John Paul II made.

PROFESSOR de PAULO: And prior to the twentieth century?

PROFESSOR KANE: No. The popes have generally steered away from making definitive statements on one side or another.

PROFESSOR de PAULO: So, Professor Tompkins brings up the controversial issue of infallibility, of course, by mentioning the *ex cathedra* statements. In this regard, if he had spoken in this way, this would have been, in your view or in the view of this panel, binding on at least all Catholics?

PROFESSOR KANE: If he were to do that. I would not have expected him to do that.

PROFESSOR de PAULO: I see. So, is it only when he speaks in this unique capacity that it is binding on the consciences of Catholics?

PROFESSOR KANE: That is a broad question. I mean, you are looking at the exercise of the "extraordinary magisterium" in terms of making a definitive statement about something in a formulaic way: *ex cathedra* versus the teaching of the "ordinary magisterium" of the Church throughout the tradition. And certainly there is a role for that ordinary magisterium, but on the level of making particular judgments about particular conflicts, I do not think you are apt to find a great deal of consensus among Catholic theologians or Catholics in general saying this one definitive position.

PROFESSOR de PAULO: Now, constitutionally, Professor Kane, where is the authority in the Roman Catholic Church? Is it in the professors of philosophy and theology, collectively in our universities, or is it in the college of bishops; and does it reside in the papacy?

PROFESSOR KANE: It is within the Church; it rests with the faithful.

PROFESSOR de PAULO: The faithful?

PROFESSOR KANE: And then the structure of the Church exercises that authority through the pope and the bishops.

PROFESSOR MARGOLIS: There is a paradox here that seems to me to be absolutely essential. If the judgment is construed as a finding of reason, then it can't be the case that the pope has supreme authority. Wait a moment. . .that is part of it. If he has supreme authority with respect to the Catholic world in whatever sense you interpret it, it can't be a finding of reason, all right? That, I think, is one paradox I see no way of solving.

PROFESSOR de PAULO: This is a theoretical and speculative point. Canon law, however, is not so speculative; Canon law is very clear, just like the law of any country.

PROFESSOR MARGOLIS: Right. But the history of reason as a cognitive faculty has been challenged in an increasingly powerful way.

PROFESSOR de PAULO: I see. So are you suggesting that. . .I mean, you agree, you said, with His late Holiness' view on the war?

PROFESSOR MARGOLIS: No, no, I agree with his judgment, but not with the validity of the reasons.

PROFESSOR VAN FLETEREN: Necessarily?

PROFESSOR MARGOLIS: In terms of who makes the judgment.

PROFESSOR de PAULO: Let me ask you, for a Catholic, if the pope's statements are made within the ordinary magisterium – and for the sake of the record, that includes, in your opinion, encyclicals, apostolic letters, anything else?

PROFESSOR KANE: The tradition includes not only formal papal statements, but to a certain extent, the statements of bishops and, in fact, the statements of Catholics; in general, they are all part of it.

PROFESSOR de PAULO: The United States Conference of Catholic Bishops collectively said the war was unjust, which is in union with Rome; so that is a Catholic position. Is that binding on the consciences of Catholics according to Canon law or moral theology?

PROFESSOR KANE: In what sense do you mean binding on the consciences; in other words, you have to definitively hold that position?

PROFESSOR de PAULO: That if these are formed consciences . . .

PROFESSOR VAN FLETEREN: You have to definitively hold that position.

PROFESSOR de PAULO: No, if they have formed consciences. They, I guess, would have to assent to this position.

PROFESSOR KANE: No.

PROFESSOR de PAULO: In your estimation, no?

PROFFESSOR MARGOLIS: In my estimation, not either.

PROFESSOR VAN FLETEREN: I think these are matters for theological and philosophical discussion.

PROFESSOR de PAULO: That is what we are holding. That is what tonight is about.

PROFESSOR VAN FLETEREN: Tonight so far has been about the papal authority, that is what tonight has been about so far, and I mean, we can discuss papal authority, if you like, but I do not think it is the topic for this evening, and I do not think it is appropriate.

PROFESSOR de PAULO: Fred, with all respect, I am the organizer of this event, and I have to tell you that it is pertinent to this book that I am writing and you are contributing to, and it is pertinent to this discussion. In part, because in the symposium previously held, some of what came out was that distinctions were being made, I suppose, to avoid the controversial issue of conscience. I am not seeking whether or not these statements were *ex cathedra*, I think it is clear that they were not. If they were part of the ordinary magisterium, this is a question that intrigues me and I think is very relevant, because we have Catholic soldiers that are fighting in this war. And if the pope's view is that this is unjust, and that was part of an ordinary magisterium, that was told to us all over the media and through the Nuncio, etc, and if these Catholic soldiers had formed consciences, is it possible that they can go to war with a clean conscience?

PROFESSOR KANE: Certainly.

PROFESSOR de PAULO: Certainly?

PROFESSOR KANE: I think that the statements of the bishops and the pope are meant to clarify the issue, but they were not statements to be held definitively; although, I would agree with their conclusions. I think that, you know, it is a difference of emphasis. I mean, certainly, my own position would be that if you carefully understood these statements, you would come to the same conclusion, but they are not statements which are meant to invoke obedience and moral thought.

PROFESSOR MARGOLIS: Isn't this problem right at the heart of Augustine's original position?

PROFESSOR VAN FLETEREN: What do you mean?

PROFESSOR MARGOLIS: I mean that the very engagement in war is, in fact, a failure of a moral kind; on the other hand, there is a problem of . . .

PROFESSOR VAN FLETEREN: I do not think only Augustine would hold that.

PROFESSOR MARGOLIS: No, no, but I take it in my weak way of mastering the tradition, Augustine is the first important voice on this particular thesis that the question of war for the human condition, in some way, just allows the condemnation...so to say, of engaging in war. There must be some commensurability between the provocation for entering a war and the condition under which human beings face it. But one strand in the Augustinian line, if I understand it correctly, is that in some way, there is no satisfactory indication of war, because it involves the slaughter of human lives in which it does. Am I wrong about that?

PROFESSOR VAN FLETEREN: I think you have to nuance that a bit.

PROFESSOR MARGOLIS: I am prepared to change my view.

PROFESSOR VAN FLETEREN: Are you talking about historical view or are talking about . . .

PROFESSOR MARGOLIS: No, no, historical. I don't . . .

PROFESSOR VAN FLETEREN: What I mean is, I think he said that some wars are justified, and there is the passage from which Thomas Aquinas cites from the *Contra Faustum*, which I think...I think it's the twenty second book of the *Contra Faustum*. . .and what he is trying to do there is against the Manicheans, who did not like Old Testament authority. And one of the things they stated is, well, look at the wars of Moses; how can you possibly uphold the Old Testament; and Augustine was saying, well, look, there are some wars that are justified, and one of the things that justifies war is a proper authority, one is just cause and one is right intention. So, I mean, I do not think it is true to say that he had a…condemnation of war; did he like it? He did not like it.

PROFESSOR MARGOLIS: I see your point and, in a way, I take it that is, in fact, very much the way in which John Paul II had seen the problem when he said war is itself evidence of moral failure. And I think that this theme is a genuine theme.

PROFESSOR de PAULO: Professor Messina will be taking up the traditional criteria in the second session. And, perhaps, we have exhausted the issue of papal authority for this table? One of the questions, and a much broader question that Professor Margolis touched upon, would be the problem of religious versus secular authority. Would you speak on this topic?

PROFESSOR MARGOLIS: Me?

PROFESSOR de PAULO: Any one at this table.

PROFESSOR MARGOLIS: All right. I will try to formulate a few dictates, if I may call them that. One is that there is no such thing as a science of morality; this is, I know, a thesis that the Catholic world would disagree with entirely. I am aware of that.

PROFESSOR de PAULO: And Professor Van Fleteren would lose a job.

PROFESSOR VAN FLETEREN: I would take another job. (laughter).

PROFESSOR TOMPKINS: Change your title. (laughter).

PROFESSOR de PAULO: But go on.

PROFESSOR MARGOLIS: There is, as far as I can make out, no way of demonstrating that morality is, in any sense, the subject of a rational science, okay? That is one thesis. That does not mean that moralities can't be reasonable. However, I think I agree that they can be reasonable in terms of the received traditions of how human beings have faced and solved these problems. But I think that it is consistent with that, that there is no evidence of a clear convergence on the part of the people of the world towards some reasonably extractable idealized conception that the entire tradition is moving toward. I don't see any evidence of that.

PROFESSOR de PAULO: How about religious versus secular authority?

PROFESSOR MARGOLIS: Second point: I have two formulations; I hope you will allow me. One is that reason has no reason to have faith in faith, and faith has no reason to have faith in reason, and that there is no evidence for reasons that are parallel to what I was saying before: that faith and reason can be counted on to be compatible, okay? I think there is clear evidence. . .well, one might say, look, in the Muslim world, it is clearer from the non-Muslim world that there is no convergence between faith and reason, and from the Muslim world, the same thing is true of the Christian world. Okay?

The seculars are in exactly the same position in a reduced way. They do not have the resources of faith to appeal to, but there is no evidence that rational discussion of morality around the world has ever moved in a single or convergent direction. And I think, myself, that the problem of international peace, just war – if you want to put it in other things of that kind – has to do with finding a rational way of reconciling incompatible views. It is the contest of partisans that is the nature of our conflict today. It is not the application of a valid position, which people around the world simply have not grasped, that can't be shown.

PROFESSOR de PAULO: In your estimation . . .

PROFESSOR MARGOLIS: I am putting it flatly.

PROFESSOR KANE: I would say I agree with you up until about the last three sentences in which I would simply add that I think that as you are saying reason and faith, seculars themselves have a kind of faith claim. And so I think that part of the difficulty is the incommensurability of different faith systems, whether we are talking about Islam or Christianity. And part of the way in which I think just war theory has worked over time is particularly because of that...somewhat of a consensus, at least, about a normative grounding for how we make these decisions.

PROFESSOR MARGOLIS: Yes.

PROFESSOR KANE: And the place of state...state craft within a religious tradition in which it makes sense. A perfect example, I think, is the whole attempt by the American government to have the Iraqis form a constitution. And the original constitution included the denial of rights to women, at which point, the American government said, well, you can't do that. But if we believe in self-determination, it would seem that that would be perfectly acceptable, but it violates the very principles of democratic government.

PROFESSOR MARGOLIS: Right; and the Americans are now embarrassed by this whole thing.

PROFESSOR KANE: But I think democracy, again, presumes a kind of epistemology that you have to agree to, and that if you do not have that common foundation, you end up, again, in incommensurable places.

PROFESSOR MARGOLIS: I would not say "epistemology," but a certain sense of acceptable procedures, which have a strong consensual basis. That, I think, is extremely problematic. I see no reason to believe that that is true.

PROFESSOR de PAULO: Professor Van Fleteren?

PROFESSOR VAN FLETEREN: Now we are getting into questions about epistemology?

PROFESSOR TOMPKINS: Joe [Joseph Margolis] is here. When Joe is here, epistemology is on the table.

(Laughter).

PROFESSOR VAN FLETEREN: And about what you said, I would like to make three or four comments, if I could? The first is about the convergence between faith and reason; that has been an error of the problem: that they were making attempts on this line. The second thing is, it seems to me, that you could use another criterion for truth besides convergence. I mean, it would seem to me, I would think that there is some kind of immutable truth. I could cite a few for you if you would like?

PROFESSOR MARGOLIS: I would like.

PROFESSOR VAN FLETEREN: The law of the distributed middle: the middle term of a syllogism must be distributed at least once. For example, I would say also that a thing is what it *is*; that the whole is greater than its parts, and I think there are a lot of truths, but anyhow, all I am suggesting is. . .you asked me to give examples, so I gave an example. Some of those are from

[Augustine's] *De Magistro*…but I do not think convergence is necessary for the criteria of truth. So maybe…well, I guess we can leave it there. If we want to, we can reduce every question to the epistemological question.

PROFESSOR MARGOLIS: No, I did not mean to. I am sorry; I did not really mean to do that.

PROFESSOR de PAULO: We accept your apologies.

(Laughter).

PROFESSOR MARGOLIS: I was looking at it in terms of the political dimension.

PROFESSOR de PAULO: Thank you.

PROFESSOR MARGOLIS: That we have important bodies of people who are in mortal conflict with one another.

PROFESSOR VAN FLETEREN: No doubt.

PROFESSOR MARGOLIS: And shall we grant their sincerity on every possible scale within reason? And they – I think we can say politically – cannot come to a resolution, in any way, that is based on the kind of pursuit of the inquiry in some decent way. And I think we see that the world sees itself moving in the direction of increasing danger and one says, look, we may not agree, but we would like to put a stop to this or slow it down in some way. Now, I think there are rational ways of doing that, but they do not take the form of applying the science of morality. Roughly, that would be my position.

PROFESSOR VAN FLETEREN: Because there isn't any such thing?

PROFESSOR MARGOLIS: I do not think that there is.

PROFESSOR de PAULO: Thank you. Professor Tompkins?

PROFESSOR TOMPKINS: I just have a footnote: in terms of practice, there are multiple opportunities for convergence. There is the hostility within Islam between different parties. Is justice fierce, if not fiercer than the hostility between Islam and the West and the fabled clash of civilizations model? Hostility in the West, among various Christians in the Church even, is pretty fierce.

PROFESSOR MARGOLIS: I agree with you.

PROFESSOR TOMPKINS: And there are standards by which communities have established practices – notice I am not talking about morality and science – that converge every day. I mean, the

Qur'an is full of admonitions toward just warfare and just treatment of non-combatants, which from the point of view of seventh century Islam, looked pretty advanced. And the communities can converge around areas of agreement between the interpreted community.

PROFESSOR MARGOLIS: I agree with that. That is exactly the kind of thing I am talking about. I think what we can't have, and here I press the point along the lines that Fred [Van Fleteren] has mentioned, there is no way to show that this will lead to universal consensus; that is the problem. You can have strategies, which lead to working solutions. I mean, I will give you an example, which I think is a good one. Granted, the stalemate in Israel between the Israelis and the Palestinians, both sides are fed up with the war; they do not know how to solve it, but there may be *ad hoc* solutions, one hopes, that will reduce the chaos there, but it will not solve the universal problem which seems to lie behind so much of our thinking. And I think that the answer is, partly, we should abandon trying to resolve the universal questions – not abandon them, but we should hold them in the wings in a sense and get on with these more moderate solutions.

PROFESSOR de PAULO: Thank you. I want to return to the question at hand. It looked like Professor Van Fleteren had a comment before you gave your example.

PROFESSOR VAN FLETEREN: Well, I was just saying, I think the solution to these things is partially because of the application of universal principles to the particular areas. I mean, that is the first thing. The second thing is I do see – and I think I may agree with you on this point – it seems to me that there is a rational attempt to come to grips with problems. I think that is a good thing rather than a bad thing. And we should not give up on hope that there is such thing as coming to a conclusion or coming to a convergence, right? You should not give up that hope, right? Even though I do agree that we all are plagued with ignorance and all that sort of thing.

PROFESSOR de PAULO: Thank you. Anyone else on this topic of religion versus secular authority?…any final statement?

Okay. I neglected to permit you an opening statement. So, let me allow you a closing statement to the first session. Can I begin with Professor Tompkins?

PROFESSOR TOMPKINS: Just briefly, I found this extremely informative. I have learned, certainly, details about thinking within the Church that I did not know about. And Joe Margolis has opened horizons for me, so I am very grateful.

PROFESSOR de PAULO: Thank you. Professor Margolis?

PROFESSOR MARGOLIS: I think that middle-sized questions like the question of just war and terrorism...

PROFESSOR VAN FLETEREN: That is a middle-sized question?

PROFESSOR MARGOLIS: Middle-sized questions.

PROFESSOR VAN FLETEREN: I was not sure I heard you correctly.

PROFESSOR MARGOLIS: What I meant by that was middle-sized . . .

PROFESSOR VAN FLETEREN: Not at all.

PROFESSOR MARGOLIS: There are working conceptions applied to familiar and concrete situations without rising to the level of first principles or something of that kind. That, I think, is a viable and important thing. My sense is that, given that way of looking at it, the discussion of just war and the discussion of terrorism is in shambles right now, and I think part of the reason is, first of all, no one has a really promising way of relating systematically the analysis of terrorism to the analysis of war in terms of the just war traditions. I do not believe that there is any sustained account of terrorism in those terms, and I think that it challenges us because it forces us to see that a kind of wholesale slaughter, which terrorism and new fangled forms of warfare now are, shall I say, in effect, is tolerated for purposes of discussing justice in warfare in a way which was never true in the Modern era before now. And that means that the just war theory, if it were revived, has to be radically reformed in terms of this kind of slippage. That, I think, is an absolutely crucial conversation. I will stop there. I think there are other things to be said, but that, I think, is the key point.

PROFESSOR de PAULO: You will have an opportunity to pursue this in the next session. But any other remarks on anything that we discussed that you want to . . .

PROFESSOR MARGOLIS: Well, I can only admit that I am an ignoramus. Many of the details of the Catholic [just war] theory and practice and the structure of the Church, which I would, myself, be very glad to be better informed on...I am with Dan [Daniel Tompkins] on this particular point.

PROFESSOR de PAULO: Professor Kane?

PROFESSOR KANE: The difficulty today is that we have, in a sense, a political system, which has been formed by the remnants of a certain way of thinking about states, and that on one very pragmatic level, there is a need for consensus. I mean, your middle term principle [referring to Professor Van Fleteren], I think, makes a lot of sense. On one level, toleration and consensus are essential components of diplomacy and of establishing some sort of justice within the international sphere. The difficulty, I think, is that toleration and consensus are themselves rooted in certain kinds of foundational beliefs. And so, on one level, I think we have to forgo that conversation of first principles. On another level, however, we are rapidly facing the situation – terrorism is a good example of this – in which it [*i.e.*, terrorism] refutes the very foundations of state craft, and I do not think that that leads us towards the realm of not being able to discuss this, but almost to a point where we have to insist upon certain kinds of ideas as being essential for any sort of international community. I am thinking about the situation that just played out in the past week in terms of the Afghani man who was brought to trial for being a Christian and was condemned to death. I think that, in some ways, Islam, as a religion, is less tolerant of that religious liberty than Christianity is. And if you look at Western culture and development and adjust it to our theory, it presumes certain kinds of beliefs, which, although we do not lay them out on the table, are essential for the final ability of just war theory to mediate different claims between states. And that is where we are at in terms of [just war theory]: we have the remnants, the language, but not necessarily the consensus about the foundations for the application of this.

PROFESSOR de PAULO: Thank you. Professor Van Fleteren?

PROFESSOR VAN FLETEREN: I will tell you the things that I would like to have discussed here, things that we might be able to learn from the present situation. I would like to have some kind of discussion about the just authority for war. I think that is a really good point.

PROFESSOR de PAULO: In the next session…

PROFESSOR VAN FLETEREN: The second thing, I was really, really looking forward to some kind of discussion about preemptive strike or preemptive war, because it seems to me that that is an important point. And the third thing – and this has come up relatively recently, I think – they used to talk about a right to war, *jus ad bellum*, the right in war, *jus in bello*, and now, in the last twenty five years, we talked about the *jus post bellum*, right? And I would like to see some discussion of that, because I do not know there are any real principles that have considered this part of the just war theory, so I think that it is a good thing to discuss. And I would give you the example, after the First World War, we seem to have made a perfectly awful peace; and then after the Second World War, we seem to have made also a perfectly awful peace, right? And we are still fighting the outcome of the First World War, and in some of the parts of the world the Second World War. So that, I think, maybe if we could talk a little about that, you know, what rights there are and what we should be doing about it. See, there is a big criticism of George Bush that he did not realize what was coming, but, of course, that has been true of every war. We did not realize what was coming after the First World War; we did not realize what was coming after the Second World War; and we did a little bit better at the end of the Second World War, but we put two hundred million people in police states, that was not, in my view, a very good solution. So, I think that we could have some discussion about that; that is probably provocative enough, right? So, I will leave it there.

PROFESSOR de PAULO: Thank you. I guess that I should have said earlier, more precisely before Professor Van Fleteren, this is following a previous symposium that actually dealt with the *jus ad bellum* questions at length. Professor Messina is going to handle that in the second session. And the idea of the preemptive strike came up in the previous symposium. I did not give you the transcript of that because I did not want you to respond to their statements, but you will have the opportunity to do that.

Thank you very, very much for participating in this. And I should also introduce at this time, at least mention that Professor Steven Gale, who teaches political science at the University of Pennsylvania, is here.

PROFESSOR GALE: I do not know about political science; I know about terrorism. I would have been very happy if you had been in my course this afternoon, because we were talking about this. This is a very serious issue.

PROFESSOR de PAULO: And Mr. Gregory Montanaro is here, who is the Executive Director of the Center on Terrorism and Counter Terrorism at the Foreign Policy Research Institute at the University of Pennsylvania. And if they have questions after the second session, please feel free.

At this point, I have to conclude this session. Thank you. Let's have five minutes to stretch our legs and have a drink, and we'll reconvene.

THE SECOND SESSION

PROFESSOR MESSINA: I think that I have the unenviable task of asking you to engage in some casuistry, even though there has been some question as to whether or not such a science exists, and I hope that I will not offend you by asking you to do this.

PROFESSOR TOMPKINS: It is not a science, that's all.

PROFESSOR MESSINA: That is for another debate, perhaps. But I am forced to ask you to review at least some of the Modern, if not postmodern, interpretations or additions to the Ancient principles of just war that you rightly, I think, sourced in the thought of St. Augustine. I would like to review these quickly, you know, just to enumerate them. I have six in number here. Of course, there are varying interpretations of whether there are more or less. These refer mainly to the *ad bellum* consideration, not so much *in bello* or *post bellum*, but I think we can, certainly, cover some of that in the dialectic of our discussion, because I think it is most impossible not to, even as I now review them. So I would like to ask you to consider these, and, perhaps, give us some insight, or if you have not thought of this before, to think on your feet as to how these apply, whether or not they are even adequate for you. I mean, you could certainly address that. I am going to assume that there is some degree of adequacy, at least for the sake of conversation and that we can attempt, as Professor Van Fleteren mentioned, fueled by our own hope that somehow – and even as you said Professor Margolis – make sense out of something that seems beyond the rational, which to me, sounds like the quest for science, but nonetheless, we will let that go.

Let me just review them quickly [*i.e.*, the principles] and you let me know how you think any of these principles, either conform or violate the entrance of the war into Iraq...America's war in Iraq. And if you want to consider by contrast or by comparison, I would say Afghanistan, because that was how the original symposium was conceived, to entertain both of those wars since they came so close, one on the heels of the other, and were related to terrorism in some sense.

The first principle is legitimate authority, which I think Professor Van Fleteren said he was interested in discussing. And I think we need to discuss that, because the question is: What constitutes legitimate authority today? Certainly, in a historic context of the nation-states, it was far easier to determine that, but we do not have that luxury anymore, so I think that question should be addressed.

Also, we have the principle of just cause, that is to say whether or not the war in Iraq seemed to conform to what we understand, at least according to the twofold division of the principle: self-defense and the defense of someone weaker or a weaker nation or people.

The third, right intent, I think is the most difficult to try to assess or judge. It is hard to judge the intent of any leader who is empowered by legitimate authority to take a nation to war for whatever reason. And I think right intent is usually the Achilles' heel on nearly every war, because intentions seem to be so multifarious. If I understand Augustine right, this one has to be the strictest in terms of interpretation. Right intent has to come from a good will, a good character in the person making the decision to go to war.

The fourth is proportionality, that is, were the costs worth the benefits, and does this even apply in the American sense, since, with regard to proportionality I guess, we have such great military resource? The only question is to consider how many have died and whether that was worth fulfilling the cause in the first place, presuming that it was just?

Fifth is the reasonable expectation of success, which I think was already implied here. And I think a particular point as to whether or not this was thought out well, whether they – you know – whether it was to spread a little democracy in order to stabilize a region; whether it was – and this question has come up – a religious divide that motivated a clash of religious cultures.

And finally there is the last resort. And I guess, next to right intent, this might be the most difficult to ascertain, because how do you determine when someone should decide that all peaceful means of negotiating have been exhausted? Where do we draw the line?

So, I would like to begin by asking you to focus on any principle you find interesting, but if we could begin at the beginning with the first three ancient ones, in particular, legitimate authority. And I would ask Professor Van Fleteren, since he showed an interest in this, if he would like to say something about it.

PROFESSOR VAN FLETEREN: All right. I'll start off. I did hear it said today that the only just war is the one that is supported by the United Nations and declared by the United Nations. That may be a strong statement, but I hear that quite often; in other words, a nation-state, to use your term, by itself can't declare a war. Let me say this, but take what happened: one of the forms that it would have to take is an amendment to our [United States] constitution, because our constitution, certainly presupposes that a nation-state can do that. The second thing is, in what sense is – if it takes a sovereign state to do it – the United Nations a sovereign state? Because it does not appear to be, and I think it is Article fifty-one, or if there is someone more knowledgeable than I. . .but this is a collection; it is a collection of sovereign states. It is not, in and of itself, a sovereign state.

And so there is, at least, a big question in my mind as to whether the United Nations has the authority to declare a war?

And I would also say to you that, as I understand it, what is going on in Iraq now is supported by the United Nations. And we can ask what that means?

So, I guess I would say I do not see anything besides the notion of sovereignty, although I think the notion of sovereignty must be somewhat limited, right? I do not see anything about declaring a war except that a sovereign state could do it. And I do not think that the United Nations is a sovereign state. Now, whether we can make it into one or not is another question.

PROFESSOR MESSINA: Can I interject a question on what you said? By calling into question the authority of the United Nations, you seem to cause a problem for those who have argued that the Iraqi war seemed to have been connected to the First Gulf War, and that Iraq was responsible for violating United Nations resolutions and that this gave to them...I do not want to say an argument, but what your statement implies is that if the United Nations does not have the authority to enter into a war, then neither would these resolutions bind nor be a just cause.

PROFESSOR VAN FLETEREN: I would think that...I would hold it, because I do not think the United Nations has the power to declare war. And I do not think...I'd say...and, in fact, I would say the debacle has not made any difference, because the reason, theoretically, it cannot have any...

PROFESSOR TOMPKINS: What has made no difference?

PROFESSOR VAN FLETEREN: That the United Nations has said that there are various principles that Saddam Hussein has violated: he did not do this, or he did do that, or he did not do something else, right? And this has very little...this is now a political judgment...but it does not seem to have had much influence on anything that has happened. I do not know if you agree with that; you might disagree with that.

PROFESSOR TOMPKINS: Well, it was cited by the United States in 1941 or something like that.

PROFESSOR VAN FLETEREN: Yes, indeed, it was.

PROFESSOR MESSINA: Professor Kane, you want in on this issue of legitimate authority?

PROFESSOR KANE: Let me look at it from several different perspectives. First, I would simply say from Catholic moral theory that the definition of legitimate authority is not simply a juridical definition in the sense that the head of state has the only authority. Legitimate authority is always founded upon the purpose of the community. And let me just quote something from *Evangelium Vitae* by John Paul II in which he says, "The real purpose of civil law is to guarantee an order in social coexistence in true justice so that all may lead a quiet and peaceful life, godly and respectful in every way."[4] And so in that sense, legitimate authority is always related to the ends of the community, which is that the authority engenders that sense of justice so that everybody has the ability to become the persons who God has created them to be. So, on that level, we can look at whether or not specific persons exercise legitimate authority by going back to the foundational issues of the purpose of the community.

Now, within the United States, I think it is clear that legitimate authority to declare war is founded within the office of the president of the United States. To apply the principles specifically to the Iraq War, we have a little problem, because the justification for going to war from President Bush was precisely because Iraq had not fulfilled the mandates established by the United Nations. And so that it would seem from a purely pragmatic perspective, if the authority which had declared certain mandates to be operative was not going to act to enforce them, in a sense that the United States had tried to gather consensus from the Security Council by having other member nations agree to a consensus to do this. It was clear that they would not have that consensus. So, in what sense is the president's legitimate authority to use war for the benefit of this particular nation; how is that justly applied in the case of Iraq? I think the answer is that it is not. So, we can look at the question of whether the United Nations has the ability to declare war? I would say no. It is always derivative from the sovereignty of the states that apply it. But, particularly, when the justification being offered is that it is a violation of the United Nations mandates, it just seems to be a rather contradictory statement.

PROFESSOR MESSINA: Okay. Thank you…and Professor Margolis on legitimate authority…or any other principle that you like.

PROFESSOR MARGOLIS: Well, I look at this in a slightly different way, if I may say so. First of all, I do not think that the categories that you have offered, which are part of the tradition, stand a part from the complex trajectory of history itself, so that the meaning of those constraints undergoes a subtle change as the historical events themselves evolve. So what, for example, the meaning of sovereignty and of just cause and so on is will be an interpretation of what makes sense under the changing circumstances. The whole idea of invoking those principles, however, is that it assumes that they remain relatively changeless. But, that seems to be doubtful for all of them. I mean that the meaning of sovereignty is fantastically problematic at the present time.

PROFESSOR MESSINA: Excuse me, is this your interpretation that they are so concretized that they do not allow for further interpretation or change?

PROFESSOR MARGOLIS: Well, they allow for it, but then the interpretation gets increasingly problematic and contested. And when they are accepted with their range of application, they are accepted essentially because of consensus, may I say, largely in terms of the strong states who are willing to back that line of reasoning. I do not think the concept of just war makes any sense without the role of strong states. The reason that problem has been so serious at the present time is that the strongest of the strong states is the principle actor in the situation whose own behavior has been rendered problematic. And consequently, it is not possible to talk about the American preemptive strike, for example, in the same way that might have been possible to a lesser state. I think these are part of the realities, number one, and I think that also goes to the point of the notion of the science of morality with respect to the just war problem. I think that is the same thing.

The second point I would like to make is this: I believe that we are passing through a period of enormous political change in which it is not possible to separate the critique of peace and the critique of war. That is to say, from a certain point of view, peace is war by other means now; and that the only way to resolve these questions is to begin to think about the global conditions of an acceptable level of life for the whole human race. The lingo of the rationale for war, along these received lines, is now seen by many people to dodge the problem of the evolution of the conditions of war. So, for example, if you take the problem of the disasters in Africa, the profound inequalities of the condition of life around the world, which are not allegedly produced by war, but by peace, and say, look, what do you mean by the justification of war within a framework, which itself produces the conditions for the deep suffering of such a large part of mankind?

PROFESSOR MESSINA: You could say that right down to the individual human condition, could you not? We are the very condition of our own paradoxes.

PROFESSOR MARGOLIS: I think so. So, my point is both with respect to just war and terrorism, we have reached a point where I do not say we can't reinterpret just war, but people who are serious about this might say that you need an entirely new paradigm or model, and it must be one in which you can enlist societies around the world, or you haven't got a prayer.

PROFESSOR MESSINA: So you do not think that any of these principles are reasonable?

PROFESSOR MARGOLIS: No, no, no, they are very reasonable.

PROFESSOR MESSINA: I mean, for example, legitimate authority, when we use the term, is there something you recognize as legitimate authority in terms of a global consensus?

PROFESSOR MARGOLIS: I would say as principles, they come close to being ontological. In practice, they are problematic. And in terms of the prophecies of the future, they are outmoded. I think that is the real problem.

PROFESSOR MESSINA: Professor Tompkins?

PROFESSOR TOMPKINS: Yeah, let me say that I am not a professional, really, in the sense of being a theologian or a philosopher, but I did [appreciate] that this was an opportunity to go back and re-read chunks of Augustine, and, you know what, he is pretty good still. And the problem is he is so good that he makes most of his latter-day imitators look like pale shadows. Now, if you take the three categories you enunciated just now, authority, cause and intent, the danger in the way you have expressed them – and I thought about this as I re-read Augustine – is that they have become a sort of taxonomy of universal categories that risks being empty, almost a laundry list. And when you hear defenders of the Iraq War tote them up, it sounds like they are doing a laundry list at times. I mean, when you go to Augustine, he is wrestling with this stuff. He starts by saying you should never kill anybody, and it is the worst thing you can do. And there is this very moving part in chapter nineteen of the *City of God* where he says, any body who thinks this is easy going to war, who *humanum pirdidit sensum*, has lost his human feeling. And you can just see Augustine wrestling with this, and I am saying that. . .but to defend your flock, it is necessary, just as it is necessary to be a judge and the judge must regret being a judge every day he is a judge. So, that is what Augustine developed, and it risks becoming a bunch...do you have all six; do you have five, or do you have four and a half? I mean we have a teacher at Temple who takes his class through the Ten Commandments, and they always conclude that they follow a 2.5. So, you see this in the work of Richard Neuhaus, and you see this in the work of Jean Bethke Elshtain, who is a Protestant political philosopher at Chicago. And, you know, Stanley Hauerwas, the Protestant pacifist at Duke Divinity, who reading their work says they have converted just war theory into a sinful illusion.

And when you read, say, Neuhaus' recent statements in 2006, which are really intense, and Elshtain's also, they are partly intent on defending authority – the authority they followed to go into war. Elshtain still believes the Pentagon briefers that she is privileged to hear give her a better story – closer to the truth than the press does – even though eighty correspondents have been killed in Iraq, and even though every day brings new news that they [*i.e.*, the press] were right. And when you read Neuhaus, he almost is more critical of the pope than he is of the president. I mean, he attacks the Curia; he attacks the [U.S.] Conference of Bishops; he attacks all Catholics who disagree with him.[5] So, thinking about this, the huge burden that just war theory imposes on us, the obligation is of empiricism, getting the facts right and when you read theologians casually dabbling in matters of who has the authority of causation. I mean, causation is a pretty serious business, and intent, that it really is dispiriting. So, that is where I am.

PROFESSOR MESSINA: Well, if I may just ask a question about what you said? Is what you are saying that there is not so much a problem with the principles themselves, but the problem with interpretation? Am I reducing what you have said? Because you seem to praise the principles and you seem to want to go back to some kind of holistic way in which they originated rather than the way they have developed.

PROFESSOR TOMPKINS: I think that it is worthwhile trying to get into Augustine and see how he arrived at these principles rather than hiding behind Augustine's skirt. When I re-read the *Catechism*[6] and when I re-read every list of multiple items, and when you go online, you get underlined passages, and it takes you to sub-items and further sub-items, and it is very moving. On the fifth commandment, it is a seamless web; it starts with a need for life and then ends up with just war. And it is a real beautiful document.

I think the spirit of just war theory is really moving and wonderful, especially because it deals with real problems we all face. I think it has been violated. I think maybe it risks being violated. Pardon me for going past my time.

PROFESSOR MESSINA: Professor Van Fleteren?

PROFESSOR VAN FLETEREN: If we jettison the just war theory, I think we better come up with something to take its place.

PROFESSOR TOMPKINS: I want to jettison its advocates. (Laughter).

PROFESSOR VAN FLETEREN: Their advocates could be poor, not the documents; is that what you were saying?

PROFESSOR TOMPKINS: Yeah.

PROFESSOR VAN FLETEREN: [Turning to Margolis] You were not saying that the document itself is good, and its proponents are bad; you were saying the document itself is not worthwhile.

PROFESSOR MARGOLIS: No; I think that it is very sensible, but it is not what it is said to be.

PROFESSOR VAN FLETEREN: Okay. What do you mean?

PROFESSOR MARGOLIS: It is not a set of principles to be applied – a set of fixed principles to be applied to the changing face of war; it is a set of . . .

PROFESSOR VAN FLETEREN: But don't you think that is our job to take unchanging principles and apply them to the particular situation, and if the situation changes then . . .

PROFESSOR MARGOLIS: And the guiding interpretations change and proliferate in different directions.

PROFESSOR KANE: Then there is no constancy in terms of those principles?

PROFESSOR MARGOLIS: There is no constancy.

PROFESSOR VAN FLETEREN: They are equivocal?

PROFESSOR MESSINA: Well, I think we have come to a point of disagreement that I think, theoretically, is going to be tough to bridge. Nonetheless, I would like to forge ahead and try, if not to persuade you [*i.e.*, Margolis], because you could be the voice for the illegitimacy of the principles as we enumerate them, and others can voice their ability to apply them, if they wish.

Just cause is the next one I would like to address. With regard to Iraq and Afghanistan, either or, what is the issue with the just cause principle; how has it been applied?

PROFESSOR VAN FLETEREN: Let me start out with something here. Are you going to say the principles as they have been rhetorically presented by certain people, or are you going to tell me...or can I say what I think justifies the war?

PROFESSOR MESSINA: I think that you can say what justifies the war.[7]

PROFESSOR VAN FLETEREN: I think genocide justifies that war.

PROFESSOR MESSINA: And you are arguing that that is what is going on in Iraq?

PROFESSOR VAN FLETEREN: Yeah. I think so. You know, the low-ball figure I have heard is three hundred thousand (*i.e.*, dead); the high-ball figure is four million. I am unable to judge or anything in between, but it seems to me that that is a substantial cause, right? That would be just cause for war.

PROFESSOR MESSINA: So you are arguing that it was for the defense of others?

PROFESSOR VAN FLETEREN: I believe that that is a just cause for that war; that is what I am arguing. Now, I am not getting into the question of whose mind that was or who knew that.

PROFESSOR MESSINA: I was not asking that.

PROFESSOR VAN FLETEREN: I am saying that I think that defense of the rights of the Iraqi people to live; that would be a justification; I would say that would justify that war. And I think that overcomes, according to the document – I know it is an out-dated notion – the notion of sovereignty.

PROFESSOR MESSINA: Okay. . .Professor Kane?

PROFESSOR KANE: Just cause, as it has been used, I think, within recent history has really seen a couple of pieces added to it. Let me say that all nations recognize self-defense as a just cause. Most nations, although they have foresworn this in most of the international treaties, also recognize that there is a legitimate just cause for protecting the innocent in terms of preemptive strikes when some imminent harm will be done. I think a real problematic part of the present conflict is that the Bush Administration has added a third possibility, which is preventive; that the United States can act to prevent possible harms from occurring without specifying exactly what those are. I think that last category is, certainly not a legitimate application, because it leads to way too much leeway in terms of what you are preventing, and when is this going to happen? And the idea of preemptive means that it is rather imminent; preventive means it will occur at some time. The other piece of that, that I would add is that I think, at least, is in the articulation by the Bush Administration of what the just cause would be in this particular instance. I think that in some ways they are playing a little bit of a shell game. The argument of weapons of mass destruction, we now see, at least in retrospect, was not there. But even the argument that the violation of treaties, and some possible harm would be done to people, simply does not stand up to the facts, especially, I would say, applying it specifically to the issue in Iraq. There were United Nations weapons inspectors on the ground trying to establish whether or not there was such a thing as weapons of mass destruction, and the United States, simply, preempts all of that by saying we are simply going in. I think probably closer to the arguments, at least from an American political position is that the reason for the war was, as Paul Wolfowitz had said, oil. I think that is another self-interest.

And I do not think that reason stands up to, at least, my understanding of what just cause is.

PROFESSOR MARGOLIS: I would put the point this way: at a certain level of abstraction, the handling of the just war concept can't be separated from the interpretation of sovereignty. Given the changes in the technology of our world, I think that there will always be a *prima facie* case in favor of increasing the impact of the preemptive strike. On the face of it, that can't be knocked out of the ballpark, as far as I can see. I do not think that the United States can make a plausible case that it was, in fact, honoring that concern.

PROFESSOR MESSINA: In the case of Iraq?

PROFESSOR MARGOLIS: Yes, that is my honest opinion. But nevertheless, the idea can't really be disallowed. So, if you have a strong sense of sovereignty, then given the way the technologies are going, and now with just the last couple of days, there was, you know, this sham attempt to smuggle atomic material just as a sort of game, which succeeded both in the South and the North of the United States. Now, given that, there is going to be a rational argument of sorts, which says that we do not know exactly what the situation is, but we are worried, and who has the right to make this decision, but we, as the sovereign state, exposed because we are the strongest state in the world, etc. Now, the reality is that you can't get the rest of the world to behave in a certain way to reign in a strong state; and you can't expect that they are going to behave as judges of the validity of all of this to monitor themselves and the state that they are examining. And the result is that it becomes a kind of "catch-as-catch-can," so I think there are serious problems that are mounting for us here.

PROFESSOR MESSINA: Okay. Professor Tompkins, anything on the issue of just cause with Iraq?

PROFESSOR TOMPKINS: No. I think my previous remarks, sort of cover it.

PROFESSOR MESSINA: Okay. Professor Van Fleteren, so you want to say something?

PROFESSOR VAN FLETEREN: I just want to make a statement that I don't think that preemptive war or preventive war goes against principles of the just war theory.

PROFESSOR MESSINA: I think that he even allowed for that possibility.

PROFESSOR VAN FLETEREN: I just want to make it clear.

PROFESSOR MESSINA: Okay...let's move to the third principle then, if you don't mind, right intent, which always seems to me to be the most problematic. Was the intention of America sound on this or do issues of oil call that into question, or issues of strategic importance that have, perhaps, nothing to do with genocide or the disenfranchisement of the people or...Professor Van Fleteren, would you like to speak?

PROFESSOR VAN FLETEREN: Well, I do not know that we can really...or how we are supposed to get into the head of a head of state to figure out what his reasons were, right? There are a lot of things describing this person or that person; you can read it in the newspaper or anything like that. Let me say to you, I think that the cause of any...I would go back to Augustine on this. I would think that the cause of any war is the *libido dominandi*, the lust for power, and I think that is a pretty good example. I think that fits with Saddam Hussein "down to a T," in my view, that he had lust for power. So I can't get into judging what their motives were; who knows what they are, right? Who knows even if they know what they are, right? But this thing about oil, I certainly do not know...it seems to me...I would like somebody to give me an example of the Americans having purchased oil anywhere but on the free market. I think all our oil is purchased on the free market. I do not think there is probably a single example you can go against that. If they mean by oil that we did not want Saddam Hussein's thumb on the oil button, then I say, I think that is right. I do not think we were the only ones that did not want that; I think Western Europe would not like that either...Central Europe ...a lot of people would not like that. So, that is what I have to say on the subject.

PROFESSOR KANE: I admit it is difficult to guess at the intentions, but, certainly, there are signs that the war was disconnected from the particular pretext that was offered. Planning for the war in Iraq preceded the specific charges laid against Saddam Hussein. So, I think we can point to various kinds of actions that might give us a view of the intention. And again, I think it's not necessarily related to having the oil and just grabbing it, but I think it is also a sense of protecting a certain natural resource that we feel we should have access to. I mean, why, for instance, do we go into Iraq and not into North Korea?. . .similar regimes.

PROFESSOR VAN FLETEREN: But not similar neighbors.

PROFESSOR KANE: Nor similar resources.

PROFESSOR MESSINA: Professor Margolis, do you have anything to add?

PROFESSOR MARGOLIS: First of all, I do not think the intent is to be construed as a mental factor. It has to be public; it does not really matter what is going on in the minds of Bush and Cheyney. I think that has to be irrelevant. But it is also complicated by the fact which is another fact of life; namely, that the United States was never prepared to make public the relevant supporting evidence on the grounds that this would be dangerous to sources of information, and so on. So, there is an increasing problem of how to handle all of this in a realistic way, and I can't see how that can possibly go in any way but worse.

PROFESSOR MESSINA: Excellent. Professor Tompkins?

PROFESSOR TOMPKINS: Yeah. I have trouble judging intent, because I do not know what the president's intent was. There is increasing evidence that, certainly, the American public was misled about the president's intent. And he said up until the Spring of 2002 that he was planning no war, but the new book, *Cobra II*, as well as other journalistic releases, show that the planning began as early as 2000, right after he took office. I think that intent – the *libido dominandi* – the desire to rule, is a synonym of *cupiditas regni*, the desire to reign, and there is a wonderful passage where Augustine talks about the desire to rule, the desire to reign, which it goes on to say that this desire leads you to crush and subdue people who do you no harm. And I think it is a very legitimate question who is crushing whom; what people who did us no harm are suffering at whose hands right now, and did the president plan this; did he have the intention? I do not know. It is not quite intention, but it is really, really bad planning not to have thought ahead. I mean, we have flattened entire cities like Fallujah. When Augustine comes to the climax of this passage he says, what differentiates the state from *latrocinium*, a great highway robbery? And I think that is the question we got to keep in mind.

PROFESSOR MESSINA: That sort of segues into, I think, at least the fifth principle, and I am going to combine this and ask if any of you have a comment on these two: the reasonable expectation of success, which you seem to bring us to, was the war well thought out? Did they even know what the objective was? Were the objectives questionable to begin with, which some think is impossible to determine, or, at least dubious, and some think there are objective, determinate criteria whereby we can properly assess such objectives? But was there a reasonable expectation of success, and what was the goal if it were not oil? Professor Van Fleteren said that it was to prevent genocide; there is, perhaps, one reason. Do you have any comments on the reasonable expectation of success or whether or not we have exhausted the last resort, that is all the means of peaceful negotiation? Professor Tompkins?

PROFESSOR TOMPKINS: Well, I mean, there were, certainly, people who said it would be a cakewalk and people who kept the number of American soldiers to a minimum and people who refused to engage in phases of the planning, including the Defense Department, which rejected the whole State Department effort to plan for Iraq after the war. So, I think it is almost a joke to talk about a reasonable prospect for success.

PROFESSOR MESSINA: Anyone else who wants to comment on either the expectation of success or the last resort?

PROFESSOR MARGOLIS: There cannot have been a reasonable expectation of success if there was no analysis of the dynamics of the society that was invaded.

PROFESSOR VAN FLETEREN: What was there then?

PROFESSOR MARGOLIS: There was no knowledge of what Iraq was like, no understanding of that whatsoever in any public way.

PROFESSOR VAN FLETEREN: That may be true. It seems to me, is it not true that the country of Iraq was formed by Britain? It was formed in 1921, and it was formed quite intentionally out of these three groups.

PROFESSOR MARGOLIS: Absolutely.

PROFESSOR VAN FLETEREN: Now, it seems to me that if that is true, there must have been some knowledge of that in the British State Department, or whatever, the British Foreign Ministry; it would seem to me to be completely unrealistic to say they did not have any idea about that, as I understand it. So, it seems to me that there must have been some knowledge of that somewhere.

PROFESSOR MARGOLIS: I meant the Americans.

PROFESSOR VAN FLETEREN: Did they come and tell the Americans and the Americans rejected it?

PROFESSOR MARGOLIS: Well, I think probably ignored it.

PROFESSOR VAN FLETEREN: Well, when you say probably, this thing is so very complex to me, because I do not think you can say that the Brits, who were very much a part of this, did not understand the situation.

PROFESSOR MARGOLIS: Well, for example, there have been the analyses of the first few days and weeks of the Iraqi altercation which show that the Americans simply ignored most elementary considerations about securing the terrain in any way that would lead to whatever they wanted to do. Now, Rumsfeld[8] has certainly spoken about this in such a way that he surely confirms.

PROFESSOR VAN FLETEREN: Well, mistakes are made in war.

PROFESSOR MARGOLIS: This is not a mistake.

PROFESSOR MESSINA: This perhaps would require some more expertise in terms of the intelligence and what not.

PROFESSOR VAN FLETEREN: My point exactly.

PROFESSOR KANE: Let me just add what I would say; I do not think that the last resort was met. Clearly from what I said before, there were diplomatic negotiations going on; there were United Nations inspectors on the ground. I think there were, certainly, other ways of trying to deal with this, which is exactly what John Paul II was saying repeatedly.

PROFESSOR TOMPKINS: There was an election coming.

PROFESSOR MESSINA: May I ask one final question of the panel, then, because I am running out of time, and I would like each of you to answer, if you could. Was the war in Iraq just? Do you have a final determination in your own mind?

PROFESSOR KANE: Can you clarify your question? Are you saying was the war just prior to its initiation or according to United States government principles, or are you asking the question in hindsight as to whether the war has met the criteria?

PROFESSOR MESSINA: Well, yeah, hindsight is always 20/20, right? So let me ask you before, which is the more difficult question; was it just before the decision was made? Was it a just assessment that they should go to war?

PROFESSOR MARGOLIS: This is *ad bellum*?

PROFESSOR MESSINA: Yes.

PROFESSOR KANE: No [*i.e.*, it was not just].

PROFESSOR VAN FLETEREN: I think you can make a case for it along the lines of genocide. I think you can make a case for it.

PROFESSOR KANE: But I would add, nobody tried to make that case.

PROFESSOR VAN FLETEREN: I think that there was...the problem with genocide is as follows; in the United Nations – those people know more about it than I do – in the Charter of the United Nations, there is a proviso that says they have to intervene if there is genocide. Now, this had the effect of people getting into quibbles in the United Nations about what is genocide, right? And you get a philosophical discussion like what is going on for four or five years while the thing goes on.

PROFESSOR MESSINA: We can debate this issue...

PROFESSOR VAN FLETEREN: No, no, wait a minute; give me a chance to explain what I am saying. So, therefore, they could not use that as a justification [*i.e.*, genocide], because they never would have gotten anywhere in the United Nations, because the United Nations will never declare genocide. Therefore, they use these other grounds, but I would say that there has been in many of the speeches leading up to the second part of the Iraq war...there were many statements by the government indicating that there was a Fascist dictator there who had killed X number of thousands or millions of people, and it was not a good thing, and it justified the war.

PROFESSOR MESSINA: I understand. Professor Margolis? Was it a just war?

PROFESSOR MARGOLIS: I would say it is, in my view, a personal view, it was not just, but not in the terms of the just war theory.

PROFESSOR MESSINA: Okay...understood...Professor Tompkins?

PROFESSOR TOMPKINS: I think this is really serious business, that it is okay to ignore the facts; and what is it Neuhaus says, in the contingencies of history, we must make a postulate of ignorance? That is what he said in 2006.[9] And you know it is okay until the body count reaches a certain level. And once the body count has reached a certain level, you can't talk about ignorance, and how complicated it is, and how many facts there are involved, because people are getting killed by our ignorance. Ignorance can be a sin. If the government behaved ignorantly in that sense, it is unjust. That is enough.

PROFESSOR MESSINA: Understood. I would like to, at this point, re-introduce Professor Stephen Gale and Mr. Gregory Montanaro…

PROFESSOR de PAULO: Actually, only Professor Stephen Gale of the University of Pennsylvania has a question.

PROFESSOR MESSINA: Professor Gale?

PROFESSOR de PAULO: Just one question, if you will, to the panel, because we are going to conclude at exactly eight o'clock.

PROFESSOR GALE: I am very confused about what all of you have been talking about. According to me, my view of this theory of just war was not about preventing war; it was about achieving meaningful conclusions – victory; that is what Osama Bin Laden has done; he has used a just war theory. What is it that you conceive of the just war theory in terms of its objectivity? Is it to prevent war, or is it to get what you want in the reasonable way with reasonable expectations? You seem to be thinking of it in a very odd way from the historical theory of just war, and certainly, in the religious tradition, war was used to achieve God's will; that is exactly what Bin Laden is speaking about. So please tell me why you believe this is about preventing actions like killing people? People get killed. It happens.

PROFESSOR MESSINA: [addressing Professor Van Fleteren], Did you want to answer?

PROFESSOR VAN FLETEREN: I would just say I would take the nineteenth book of the *City of God*: "All war is waged for peace."[10] For Augustine, war is for peace. You can disagree with what I say, right? That is another question, but all war is waged for peace.

PROFESSOR MESSINA: Did anyone else wish to respond to that question?

PROFESSOR KANE: I just want to say that I think it is not victory; it is justice. It is the establishment of a just order that war is used for. So principles are used to avoid war if it is a violation of justice or to engage in war if it is an enactment of justice, so I do not see. . .I think it is an interesting question, but I do not agree with it.

PROFESSOR MESSINA: Professor Margolis, did you want to respond?

PROFESSOR MARGOLIS: I am inclined to agree with the thrust of the points made. It reminds me of the war crimes trial situation, which turns into a victorious trial, and I think it could not be anything but a victorious trial. And so I take it that what you are saying is, in fact, quite true.

PROFESSOR GALE: War happens; it is not nice.

PROFESSOR MESSINA: Professor Tompkins?

PROFESSOR TOMPKINS: There is an awful circularity to this. We have engendered huge opposition by going into Iraq; we created terrorists. The bombings in London and Madrid were staged by people who were not in Iraq, but who were emulating the terrorists in Iraq. And the trouble with talking about war bringing victory is that there is always another mountain to cross; there is always another victory you got to gain, and I do not see this war in Iraq leading to victory at all. I see it leading to more problems.

PROFESSOR MESSINA: Thank you. I would like to close this session then and thank the distinguished professors for contributing to this and to the audience for coming. I would also like to thank Professor de Paulo for organizing this wonderful event. Now, if there are any closing remarks from Professor de Paulo...

PROFESSOR de PAULO: Thank you. Thank all of you very much, and if you would join me in thanking the panel. Thank you.

Notes

[1] The Congregation of the Doctrine of the Faith is a cabinet level department of the Holy See.

[2] Michael Novak is a conservative, Catholic political writer.

[3] An *"ex cathedra"* statement refers to the pontiff's infallible teaching Office on faith and morals, proclaimed at the First Vatican Council.

[4] Pope John Paul II, *Evangelium Vitae* (Editrice Vaticana, 1995).

[5] "The Sound of Religion in a Time of War" in *First Things: A Monthly Journal of Religion and Public Life*, 133 (May 2003), 80: "officials of the Holy See, some of whom have come unconscionably close to suggesting that Catholic Americans must choose between loyalty to their country and fidelity to the Church. If, as one curial archbishop has declared, the coalition led by the U.S. is engaged in a 'crime against peace,' it would seem to follow that our soldiers are engaged in a criminal activity."

[6] *The New Catechism of the Catholic Church*, concerning Just War principles, paragraphs 2307-2317.

[7] 2003 War in Iraq.

[8] Former U.S. Secretary of Defense, Hon. Donald Rumsfeld, who served in George W. Bush's administration.

[9] "The Public Square" in *First Things*, issue 156 (October 2005): 71-87.

[10] Augustine, *City of God* XIX.3.

CHAPTER FOUR

The Future World Order: The Implications of the War in Iraq on International Law

Dieter Blumenwitz
Ukrainian Free University, Munich, Germany

T he legal culture of the world is established in notions about law and justice, but it exists also in procedural stipulations which developed in classical antiquity under the influence of the high cultures of the Persians and the Indians and continued to evolve in the history of ideas and in practice, in ambiguity and affirmation up to the present day.[1] The concept of an order, which would encompass all of humanity, emerged in the *civitas maxima* of the Greeks and Romans and in the Christian Middle Ages continued as the *civitas dei*. The deeper notion of a *lex aeterna*, an order of law superior to the times and the cultures, survived the sundering of beliefs and religious wars and extended eventually also to the New World. The latter development is attributable to the Spanish Scholastics Vitoria and Suárez as well as the Dutch Protestant Grotius, who yet during the Thirty Year's War reestablished principles of peace and war which were recognized by the combatants of the time and derived from interpretations of human nature. Classic international law, the bases of which were unchallenged in the following three centuries, established order among nations on the principle of the sovereign equality of each nation-state. War was recognized as an instrument of policy, although progressive limits were also set to the development of military power, and possibilities for the peaceful arbitration of disputes were extended. In light of this, however, ethical considerations made over the course of centuries as to when military means could be justified, the so-called *bellum iustum* principle, have made little headway in confining the use of force. Even in the relatively small circle of like-minded nations such considerations have had almost no historical effect. In their name no wars were prevented. There is the great flaw in all of this that each nation judges whether it is engaged in a just war or not, and the criteria for this are so vague that it is possible for every belligerent nation to project its war as just. Ethical notions are, thus, always liable to be degraded into elements of propaganda and national purpose. Inherent in the concept of the "just war" (*bellum iustum*) is the danger that one's own point-of-view may be made absolute. The results of this are intolerance, fanaticism and inhumanity. A peace settlement becomes all the more difficult.

The notion that a war may be both "just" or "unjust" was advanced during the age of Enlightenment: it dispenses with the notion of a "just" war and, thus, produces a basis for neutrality. This spirit of enlightenment already inspired Grotius in his three-volume text on the rights of nations, *De Iure Belli Ac Pacis Libri Tres,* which appeared for the first time in Paris in 1625; it deals with the *jus ad bellum* and also the question of preventative war: may war be waged to prevent the development of a power which could subsequently prove to be dangerous, "*ad imminuendam potentiam crescentem, quae nimium aucta nocere posset*"? Does the possibility that one may incur force, grant the right to employ force, "*vim pati posse ad vim inferendam ius tribuat*"? Grotius supplies the answer that has prevailed to this day:[2] in international law it is, however, permissible in no case, although some assert otherwise, to initiate a war in order to prevent the growth of a power which at some later date could become dangerous. I admit that in considering war this point should be taken into consideration, but not as a point of law but of practicality; so that if the war is just for other reasons, undertaking it for this reason also may be considered wise. The experts in the field assert nothing different. But the possibility that in the anticipation of experiencing force, one has the right to employ force, has no justification. Human life is constructed in such a fashion that absolute security is nowhere available. Protection from uncertain evils must be sought in divine providence or through benign guarantees, but not through force.

The peace conference called into being by Czar Nicolas in 1899 produced the agreement on the peaceful settlement of international disputes, which has existed up to today, and on the laws and customs of land warfare (The Hague Convention on Land Warfare). To be sure, the efforts of this conference were unable to prevent the two murderous world wars of the twentieth century.

THE UNITED NATIONS, THE WORLD COMMUNITY AND WAR

In order "to protect future generations from the scourge of war, which twice in our lifetime has brought unspeakable suffering to humanity," the Charter of the United Nations in 1945 ordered a universal prohibition of the use of force. All nations were obligated to refrain from the use or the threat of force in their international relations. There is no just war (*bellum iustum*) other than the war against war (*bellum contra bellum*). The "natural right of individual and collective self-defense" is, to be sure, ensured in the case of an open "armed attack." The Security Council, however, monitors all the gray areas of a military attack. It has the task to ensure that there is peace in the world. It determines whether a threat has been imposed, or a breach of the peace has transpired, or an "act of aggression" has occurred and mandates appropriate sanctions. According to its preamble, the Charter of the United Nations is not only concerned with the establishment of principles, but also seeks to "introduce procedures that guarantee that armed force is employed only in the common cause." It is the goal of the United Nations, to preserve world peace and international security, and for this purpose to employ effective collective measures. The priority is to employ peaceful means in accordance with the principles of justice and international law (Article 1 Number 1 UN Charter).

In the collective security system of the UNO, for the first time – even if only in germination – there is the solution to one of the fundamental problems of the world's nations: *Quis judicabit?* – the application and the enforcement of law. Due to the lack of central "supranational" organs the sovereign and equal nations, up to this time, were both judge and executioner in their own cause. The application of international norms was, thus, purely a question of power. Chapter VII of the UN-Charter directed at the Security Council, from now on, disenfranchises member nations from taking unilateral action when the peace is threatened, or broken, or armed aggression has occurred.

The prohibition of war, to which already in 1928 all of the important nations had agreed in the Kellogg Pact, was for all practical purposes ineffective because the signatory nations could not agree upon a definition of aggression. In 1974, for the first time in human history, the UN-General Assembly produced a comprehensive definition of aggression, which is considered today to be part of the common law of nations. The definition of aggression does not rule – as the Hague Convention on Land Warfare was sometimes charged with doing – on legal questions pertaining to past eras. As far as international law is concerned, it is future-oriented and takes into account recent and the most recent threat scenarios: subversive military aggression unleashed by infiltrating gangs or terrorists (Article 3 Line g); indirect aggression, by permitting another nation to use one's own territory to launch an attack against a third nation (Article 3 Line f); military support for a national war of liberation (Article 7); humanitarian intervention and preventive war, with its philanthropic and euphemistic phrases (Articles 2 and 5).

The collective security of the world organization is not the expression of a self-denying pacifism; rather, it attempts also to take into account questions of power, which cannot simply be dismissed in conversation. The permanent seating of the five great powers in the Security Council and their veto rights are the price of their involvement in a system of worldwide monitoring of the peace.

It was known to the framers of the UN Charter that in the transfer of the decision-making modalities of the Great Powers that had already been set at the Yalta Conference in March of 1945 that the veto power of a super power could endanger collective

security. The Charter took this into account. The veto power reflects the function and practical reality of contemporary world order. No nation has a guarantee that the Security Council shares its
view of justice and its estimation of the actual situation and will
mandate the requested measures. The refusal to apply collective
measures of force is no more a failure on the part of the Security
Council than the use of the veto would be an infringement of justice. The Security Council's "blocking" through the action of one
or more great powers is, strictly speaking, not a malfunction. No
gaps in the normative system of international defense develop.
The universal prohibition on the use of force continues to prevail,
which prohibits nations from unilateral military action – with the
exception that they are, in fact, subject to an armed invasion. One
hundred and ninety members of the UNO are bound by international treaty to these rules of the game established in the Charter.
As obligations that arise from the UN Charter have priority over
all other international agreements, the NATO Alliance, for example, must submit to it. The statutes of the United Nations fulfill
the function of a constitution for the world community. It represents world order.

The world order newly established in 1945 on the basis of law
and concretized in institutions understood how gradually to inte-
grate the losers of the Second World War, the initially rejected
"enemy nations;" it did not disintegrate on the deep East-West
conflict, which for a while lamed the ability of UNO agencies to
act; and, not least of all, offered the large group of de-colonized
peoples a forum acceptable to all. No one had at that time thought
that the resolution of the East-West conflict could plunge the
world organization into an existential crisis. It became evident,
however, that the structures of world order were affected less by
the often referenced global opposites, for example the rich and the
poor or the free and the unfree, as they were by the group dynamics of the Super Powers. After the collapse of the Soviet Union
and the socialist camp, the USA was the only power with the potential to provide global leadership. The hope that the UNO could
establish itself in political areas which had been blocked for decades by the nations of the Warsaw Pact lasted for only a brief period of time and could, for example, resolve pressing security

questions by creating a new internal world political arrangement. In the meantime, multipolarism gave way to American unilateralism.

THE WAR OVER WAGING WAR

Hardened by the experiences of the Iraq War 1990-91 – the Security Council mandate at that time allowed the coalition of the victorious powers only to free Kuwait; it did not permit a march on Baghdad and the overthrow of the regime – the United States decided to employ the political potential unilaterally which had become available through the fall of the Eastern Block. Weakness in the face of American hegemonic internationalism and opposition to the UN General Secretary's recommended agenda for peace under auspices of the world organization became evident already in a document issued in 1992 by the American Department of Defense with the title "Defense Planning Guidance," which presented the basic principles of the new strategic military direction of American foreign policy after the collapse of the bipolar order. Where collective action does not occur and where, according to American assessments, a rapid response is required, the United States should act, in accordance with its new strategy, not only alone but, if necessary, in a preventative mode ("the U.S. should be prepared to 'preempt' the use of nuclear, biological or chemical weapons"), although the UN Charter assigns this type of guaranteeing the peace clearly to the Security Council. Chaos in international relationships would be the result if each nation unilaterally could decide on possible threat scenarios and on military measures that should be applied preventatively. The Charter's universal prohibition on the use of force would lose its meaning.

The neo-conservative strategies of American foreign and security policy took hold in Washington after the inauguration of President George W. Bush. The terrorist attacks on the World Trade Center and the Pentagon, which unleashed worldwide horror and concern, accelerated the process. The United States no longer distinguished between the terrorists who had perpetrated the attacks and the countries that have apparently given them shelter. Thus, the war against Afghanistan, against Iraq as well as other so-called "rouge states" was announced and the rule of order governing nations that had existed up to that time was pushed aside.

War as a concept of justice existing between nations is related to nations and to places and cannot be extended into infinity. Terrorists are common criminals not war lords; they are neither legal nor illegal combatants. Also multiple murder is *prima facie* an act punishable according to the code of justice that exists among nations; it is not a "military attack" in the sense of Article 51 of the UN Charter. In the case of September 11th, it is even doubtful that, according to conventional measures, one may speak of "external force," because the terrorists passed through controls when they entered the United States, maintained legal residence there, acquired the necessary flight-technical knowledge and access to civil aircraft there, which were then employed as "weapons." In the case of such intensive domestic involvement, the law of nations requires that the affected nation will protect itself through suitable internal controls. The level of an "act of aggression" is only reached when a foreign nation has intentionally "sent in" terrorists to perpetrate actions, that in accordance with their level of intensity are comparable to a military attack (Article 3 Line g definition of aggression). The "sending in" of terrorists by a nation in order to conduct a covert "subversive" attack has a different quality about it than simply "providing safe haven."

THE *PAX AMERICANA* AND THE LOGIC OF IMPERIAL POWER

The war against Iraq, initiated by the United States, has found many partially contradictory legal explanations. In the final analysis, the United States claims a right to "preemptive actions." America may not only conduct war if it is attacked militarily but if it feels itself directly threatened ("imminent threat"). In the case of so-called rogue states even the mere possibility that they could at some time employ weapons of mass destruction is considered to be a threat. The new war strategy was, additionally, decked out with philanthropic considerations: the Iraqi people must be freed from a tyrannical regime.

The removal of the government of a country, neither according to classical philosophy of law nor according to the international law, is a permissible goal of war. The attempt to free a people often only brings chaos to a population and new tyrannies. Therefore, the definition of aggression only permits support for an already existing national freedom movement not, however, the installation of a puppet government through military might.

Nonetheless, the fall of the Iraqi dictator and his power apparatus, which destroyed human lives, could incontestably be a step in the right direction, which in the eyes of the world legitimizes the employment of illegal means, at least *ex post*. Must not the procedural considerations and processes of the UN Charter not take a back seat, if it is a matter of the realization of a greater good, such as basic human rights? Should one not, at least, weigh the balance between the prohibition against the use of force, on the one hand, and the protection of human rights, on the other, to guarantee uniformity in the management of the rights of nations (border questions of justice and morality, which the Kosovo conflict had already made clear?) For the general public and often also for politicians, the factual matters and the postulated legal situation are in the foreground. The task of the science of international law, on the other hand, is to maintain procedural rationality. The wide-reaching economic, social, and human rights issues can only be realized if the constitutional bases of international order, of which the universal prohibition on the use of force and its narrowly circumscribed exceptions are a part, are taken into consideration. The continuing suppression of permitted military force in international relationships is to be counted among the great achievements of civilization. The goal of a just peace in a Kantian sense can only be achieved if moral rigor, when the individual ethics of a greater good finds its limits in the establishment of decision-making conditions consistent with the rights of nations, is in the procedural control of the Security Council. Otherwise humanitarian selflessness is in danger of being subordinated to the logic of imperial power.

The reasons, which the American side has offered for the Iraq War, make clear the current liaison between two controversial neo-conservative schools of thought, which determine political life in Washington: the "Structuralists," led by the Deputy Secretary of Defense, Paul Wolfowitz, seek in the new American century ("Project for the New American Century") the democratic trans-formation of the entire Middle East, in an American sense. Then Vice-President Dick Cheney and the Secretary of Defense, Donald Rumsfeld, are to be counted among the "Interventionists," who would rather have a rapid withdrawal of Americans once the threat to the global dominance of Washington, in a strategically important region, has been turned aside. It is, therefore, still an open question whether the new unilateralism will produce only an expansion of American power or if it will lead to an all-encompassing *Pax Americana*, to the benevolent hegemony of Washington. The changes in the structure of international coex-istence are dramatic. Is the arrangement between nations reestab-lished after 1945 with so much toil in ruins?

The legitimizing principle of legal parity is lacking for the fu-ture. With due consideration the UN charter lists the "sovereign equality of all of its members" in primary positions, namely in Article 1 Number 2 and Article 2 Number 1. International law is the law of free people with equal rights. It assumes the existence of multiple sovereign nations, which recognize each other as equal partners within a community. That this "International Law of the States" could not simply be replaced by the "cosmopolitan law of a society of world citizens," philosopher Jürgen Habermas recog-nized in the short step from Kosovo to Iraq. The norms of a world order, which have developed over more than two millennia can preserve their law making power only if Washington's unilateral-ism is replaced by a new multipolarity. The signs of the times, to be sure, are not very encouraging.

Europe has sacrificed the integration depth, which would have been able to provide a common foreign and security policy, in fa-vor of an integration breadth, *i.e.*, the continuing acceptance of more and more new nations. European unity has, therefore, stag-nated for years at the level of a qualified free trade zone, a "late-Venetian merchant republic" without its own foreign political muscle. Russia needs, at least, two decades to be able to play once again the role of a somewhat equal partner to the United States. China needs the same period of time to develop into an uncontested super power. In the next decade both nations in their development are more reliant upon the USA than Europe.

The responsibility of the Security Council for world peace clearly established in the Charter, and American hegemonic claims can hardly be reconciled. In the efforts which have already been announced to bring UNO and the USA closer together, the world organization has to be wary not to be used by the sole super power and, thus, be marginalized. Because of the American veto power in the Security Council, the UNO, for its part, cannot have a direct influence upon Washington. In the foreseeable future only one hope remains: the American civil society, which is less imperial and martial in its orientation than the neo-conservative strategists of the former Bush administration and which has not yet lost its normative authority.

Notes

[1] Translated from *Die Zukunft Der Weltordnung; Zu den völkerrechtlichen Implikationen des Irak-Kriegs,* Ukrainian Free University, Varia no. 49, Munich (2004) by Bernhardt Blumenthal, La Salle University.

[2] Hugo Grotius, *De jure belli ac pacis libri tres,* Paris 1625, Lib. II, Cap. 1, § XVII: *"Illud vero minime ferendum est quod quidam tradiderunt, iure gentium arma recte fümi ad imminuendam potentiam crescentem, quae nimium aucta nocere posset. Fateor in consuktationem de bello & hoc vinire, non sub ratione justi, sed sub ratione utilis: ut si ex alia causa justem sit bellum, ex hac causa prudenter quoque susceptumjudicetur: nec aliud dicunt qui in hanc rem citantur auctores. Sed ut vim pati posse ad vim inferendam jus tribuat, ab omni aequitatis ratione adhorret. Ita vita humana est, ut plena securitas nunquam nobis constet. Adversus incertos metus à divina providentia, & ab innoxia cautione, non à vi praesidium petendum est."* Translation by Walter Schätzel, *Die Klassiker des Völkerrechts,* vol. 1 (1950), 145.

CHAPTER FIVE

The Question of Just War Theory and the Augustinian *Caveat Praeemptor*

Daniel P. Tompkins
Temple University

C an wars be just? Some Christians believe not, and have maintained a fundamental commitment to pacifism. On the other hand, many Christians use "justice" both as a motive for war and a guide to conduct in combat. "Just war theology" has until recently focused on the first of these, the right to go to war (*ius ad bellum*), with behavior in war (*ius in bello*) as at best an afterthought: the golden age of just war theology, from 1250-1650, was notorious for violence against noncombatants. In the past sixty years, however, the Vatican, the U. S. Catholic bishops and the *Catechism of the Catholic Church* have begun to emphasize other restrictions on going to war, eliciting loud protests from the "just war theologians" discussed in this essay.[1]

Meditations on justice in warfare, of course, predate Christianity, as my colleagues state in Chapter One. Among the ancient Romans, Cicero left a body of reflections on appropriate military action. In 44 BC, he influenced later thinkers by saying, "We go to war so as to live unharmed in peace." The Romans, he noted, conferred citizenship on some vanquished adversaries, while totally destroying others. He adds a word of "regret" for Corinth: "I wish we'd not razed it, but I think we had a reason – perhaps the location." Less than a decade before he wrote, Julius Caesar had imposed Roman rule on Gaul, exterminating hundreds of thousands of non-combatants. Cicero, we will find, was not the only theorist of just combat to seem remote from contemporary military practice. [2]

The Christian tradition from the outset focused on military leadership and the duty of the Christian in war. St. Paul marshaled imperatives and deployed military metaphors to portray God as commander-in-chief, passing orders down the line:

> Let every person be subject to the governing authorities. For there is no authority except from God, and those that exist have been instituted by God. Therefore he who resists the authorities resists what God has appointed, and those who resist will incur judgment. [3]

Paul's advice jars even more than Cicero's considering his circumstances. Jerusalem, his destination as he wrote, would be within a decade horribly sacked by the men he called "God's servants for your good." These "servants of God" would, moreover, have Paul arrested in Jerusalem, bring him to Rome, and very likely order his execution. [4] These ironies do not diminish Paul's own authority. In fact, his restriction of military control to a formally selected sovereign directly influenced Augustine and Aquinas, and very likely, later secular rulers.

Paul's ideal ruler is no selfish solo actor, but the protector of a community, a *neighbor*: "You shall love your neighbor as yourself." Love does no wrong to a neighbor; therefore love is the fulfilling of the law. [5] All of Paul's talk of "authority" and divine generalship, then, has the purpose of fulfilling the second great commandment; and in the Pauline tradition, war is a form of love. Following this lead, a thousand years later, therefore, St. Thomas Aquinas, following Augustine's lead, would consider warfare under the heading, *Caritas*.

We can certainly get a sense of the evolution of just war theory by taking "snapshots" at three critical moments: 1) The fifth century of the Christian era, when St. Augustine meditated on the harsh necessities of warfare, 2) The thirteenth century, when St. Thomas Aquinas drew on Augustine to formulate a rigorous "classic" triad of justifications for war, and 3) The late twentieth century, after two world wars influenced the popes and the

Church to create new standards for initiating and conducting wars. While the Augustinian tradition tolerates war, it also bristles with warnings and prohibitions that may be too seldom heeded by contemporary advocates of "just wars," including Jean Bethke Elshtain, Richard John Neuhaus, Michael Novak, James Turner Johnson, and George Weigel.[6] Today, too many theorists seem to deny the dangers that war brings, removing impediments to declaring war, and making wars of choice seem obligatory. Their success, transitory but striking, seems to have come in part from earnest compartmentalization. Suppressing the horrors of war as they touted "precision weapons," avoiding serious international relations scholarship and reading the great texts of the theological tradition with exquisite selectivity, many of today's theorists have air-brushed and marketed a lethal product.

"HUMANITARIAN INTERVENTION": GETTING CARELESS WITH *CARITAS*

Needless to say, *caritas*, or charity, plays a central role in Christian discussions, from Paul's remarks in *Romans* and Augustine's thoughts on the "obligation to love" (*necessitatem caritatis*)[7] to Aquinas and later, when Jean Bethke Elshtain invokes Augustinian *caritas* to justify unilateral warfare to rescue Iraqis she portrays as "hounded, tortured, murdered and aggrieved."[8] Though she frequently mentions Augustine and Aquinas in support of going to war, Elshtain seldom cites texts from these authors. At times, the underlying texts are difficult to locate. Further, she laces her advocacy with peculiarly hypothetical language, as when discussing "international ethics" in 2003 on National Public Radio:

> All war is a tragedy, but some could be justified if these were undertaken first to protect what he [Augustine] called the common good. In the first instance, to protect a people from slaughter and from harm....Another just occasion for the use of force might well be to protect those who are not your own nationals, to protect the innocent from harm, innocent being those who can't defend themselves who may be part of another people or a group inside another nation who are coming to harm, who are being destroyed. And at that point, an obligation of neighborly love, of *caritas* in the theological sense, might be for you to

come to their aid and to use force in order to prevent the harm that would otherwise come to these persons.[9]

"Could," "might," "would" and "if" leave us wondering: where Augustine actually endorsed Elshtain's "coercive justice," and why she neglects the violence that attends and follows armed invasion and military occupation and now dominates the news from Iraq? In the years since she spoke, Elshtain's achievement has come to appear more cosmetic than humanitarian.

In a widely-read acknowledgement of the role of "human rights" in contemporary diplomacy, Leslie Gelb and Justine Rosenthal remarked that "morality, values, ethics, universal principles—the whole panoply of ideals in international affairs that were once almost the exclusive domain of preachers and scholars—have taken root in the hearts, or at least the minds, of the American foreign policy community."[10] True, but their "panoply of ideals" is also a Pandora's box. Somalia, Haiti and Iraq, despite our "ideals," are mired in the rankings of "failed states." In Iraq, civilians have been tortured and noncombatant deaths have surged. Even if we set aside the controversial *Lancet* study, we are left with Iraqi government estimates of 150,000 dead (and that was in fall, 2006). By way of comparison, consider Darfur, where estimates start at 200,000 dead. The huge numbers beggar description, but the juxtaposition is telling. The American press routinely demonizes the agents of death in Darfur: who is responsible in Iraq?[11]

Many conservative Catholic advocates of invasion not only used Augustine carelessly, but they disregarded the growing critical literature on humanitarian intervention. The year 2003, when Gelb and Rosenthal wrote, may prove to be the high-water mark for advocacy of "humanitarian intervention." Since then, Iraq has joined Vietnam and Waterloo as shorthand for military disaster, and "humanitarian intervention" is itself under assault.

In the past decade, we have become increasingly aware of the danger of isolating "human rights" from their historical context. A wide-ranging indictment of Western humanitarian efforts by the Australian legal scholar Anne Orford reminds us that self-proclaimed "saviors" often bring about the human rights problems they seek to solve. Orford mentions the International Mone-

tary Fund's "shock therapy" in the former Yugoslavia, which removed buffers that allowed or supported inter-ethnic cooperation.[12] Other examples include the United States' support for
Mujahedeen and bin Laden in Afghanistan in the 1980's; for Saddam Hussein even when he was using "weapons of mass destruction" against Iranians and Iraqi Kurds in the 1980's; and for
the Said Barre government in Somalia (as long as the Cold War
was underway). The mixed goals of military intervention can
contradict or undercut its "humane" pretension. Our incursion in
Iraq, we now learn, was expected to benefit the United States in
the form of natural resources and massive long-term bases. David
Halberstam reveals the generally mixed motives in other situations in *War in a Time of Peace: Bush, Clinton, and the Generals*, describing the complex decision-making behind American decisions
about Bosnia, Somalia, Haiti, Kosovo and of course Rwanda. Of
these, only Bosnia seems today to count as a success. Sadly, in my
opinion, there is no sign at all, even in their recent work, that
Elshtain, Weigel, Neuhaus and Novak considered the complex
aetiology of human rights problems, or the frequently tragic consequences of intervention.

PRE-WESTPHALIAN, PRE-LAPSARIAN?

The Peace of Westphalia, concluded in 1648, which helped to
create the modern European state system. It asserted the ruler's
authority within a territory, prohibited outside interference, and
removed religion from the realm of international politics. Criti-
cizing it but ignoring the context, opponents of the Peace engage
in historical hopscotch. George Weigel pronounces Westphalia ineffective against "rogue states"; James Turner Johnson finds it
"morally sterile"; Elshtain prefers Christian "coercive justice" to
Westphalia's respect for state borders. We recall Pope Innocent X's
description of the Peace as "null, void, invalid, iniquitous, unjust,
damnable, reprobate, inane, empty of meaning and effect for all
time." Enshrining herself on a theological Rushmore, Elshtain
claims to represent "the theological tradition of the great pre-
Westphalians: Augustine, Aquinas, Luther, and Calvin": as if this
Peace, which helped to end a horrid religious conflict, marked not

a diplomatic achievement but a fall from grace, and as if the Thirty Year's War was Edenic.[13]

No one, of course, waves a wand and brings immediate historical change. Daniel Philpott's *Revolutions in Sovereignty: How Ideas Shaped Modern International Relations* gives a nuanced version of the prehistory and outcomes of the Peace.[14] Certainly, Augustine and other ancients show that state sovereignty was not invented in 1648, as the just war theologians imply. As T. M. Parker told us in 1955, Augustine reflects an ancient tradition of "indivisible unitary sovereignty" that only later receded before the "Medieval conception of the state as *societas societatum*" or society of societies.[15] St. Augustine's *City of God* respects the national borders Elshtain holds in such low regard. To start with, Augustine insists that order is central to an organized community, and that a strong and legitimate sovereign leader acts out of love for his own people. In Book 19, with its shepherds, kings, and righteous leaders, and its attention to the properly ordered household and city, Augustine envisions a sovereign state undisturbed by cross-border incursions.

Indeed, Elshtain herself nowhere challenges this notion of a good community, nor does George Weigel ever criticize the Lateran Treaty of 1929, which confirmed the state sovereignty on which the Vatican regularly relies. These authors do not desire universal anarchy, and they want sovereignty for states they like: they just want to withhold it from states they deem "bad." In this sense they are opportunistically Westphalian, not "pre-" or "anti."

Again, it appears that Elshtain, Weigel, and their colleagues have enlisted, or interpreted, Augustine far too casually. Where, in truth, does he offer Elshtain's "presumptive case in favor of the use of armed force by a powerful state or alliance of states that have the means to intervene, to interdict, and to punish in behalf of those under assault"? She does not say. Some Augustinian apophthegms hint at possibly benign armed intervention: "By as much as the domain of lust is destroyed, by so much will that of charity be increased."[16] But "hint" is all they do. In general, the political scientist Michael Loriaux is closer to the mark when he observes that:

The Augustinian is more open than the realist to discussions of, say, intervention in the domestic politics of other nations. Inversely, however,
the Augustinian is also a lively critic of his or her own government's
right to sit in judgment.[17]

Books 14 through 19 of *The City of God* open up a vista of in-
terlaced reflections on war and *caritas*, though they provide little
support for Elshtain's positions. Emotions, the "affects and per-
turbations" (14.8-9), spring directly from "love of the good" and
"holy charity." Book 14 swarms with ambiguous moral terms:
good and bad will, love, passion and emotion: clearly we must
choose wisely, just as the old knight-protector of the holy grail
advises his visitors seeking immortality in the famous film, *Indi-
ana Jones and the Last Crusade*. Augustine emphasized that the
emotional life is central, since to lose human feeling is to lose one's
humanity, to "pay a great price of spiritual savagery and bodily
stupor."(14.9) Precisely such a loss of feeling returns in Book 19.
There, we learn that a man who views the horror of war without
sadness has "lost his human senses," and that even to wage just
wars brings mourning that such wars are needed (*The City of God*
19.7-8). Elshtain and others lead us to this strain in Augustine's
work but then, eager for combat, ignore his profound and sorrow-
ful portrayal of what war can do to us.

It might be worthwhile to view the Peace of Westphalia not as
a set of laws or even instructions but as an encoding of behaviors
that over the years have made sense. In the year 2007, we have
seen a set of examples of the achievements and failures of military
invasion and occupation. Even if these are undertaken with the
best of motives, and even when the country invaded was prostrate
with poverty, American forces have found it difficult to bring
about improvements on a scale that justifies the initial invasion:
such difficulty that one might wonder, whether "improvement"
was really the goal.

If "just war" brings such horrors, "sovereignty" makes some
sense, even, improbably, when it protects cruel rulers. This is not
because anyone approves of bad regimes, but because military
intervention may make life worse, not better, for most inhabitants,
as it has in Iraq. International borders, from this point of view, be-

come not barriers to American-sponsored "improvement" but warnings against irrational and unproductive military action.

IUS AD BELLUM; *IUS IN BELLO*: THE RIGHT TO INITIATE WAR AND COMBAT RIGHTS

As we have seen, George Weigel, James Turner Johnson and others seem to regularly find fault with contemporary, official Catholic formulations about war. Their targets have included the American bishops' statement of 1983 (*The Challenge of Peace*), various recommendations from the Vatican, and the official *Catechism of the Catholic Church*, promulgated by Pope John Paul II. All these are pilloried for replacing the "classic," "principled" or "traditional" justifications of war with "modern" and "prudential" concerns. The "classic" version, we are told, starts with the three "deontological" bases of just war, as outlined by Aquinas in *Summa Theologica* (2.2.40): 1) Sovereign authority within a state (*auctoritas principis*), 2) Just cause (*causa iusta*) and 3) Right intention (*intentio recta*). The *Catechism* reduces these causes to a single one: "self-defense" (2308). There seems to be very little available documentation explaining this concentration on a single source or cause, but Catholic theologian John Courtney Murray in 1960 traced it to Pope Pius XII. According to Murray, Pius XII held to the basic position that "all wars of aggression, whether just or unjust, fall under the ban of moral proscription." In Murray's view, this is a basically Augustinian position going back to the principle of *causa iusta*, and grew out of Pius' twin beliefs that modern war is intolerably violent, and that any aggression impedes the development of international controls of war.[18]

The "prudential" reasons for war, which were developed after Aquinas and which so irritate the "just war theologians," are found in *Catechism* paragraph 2309:

1. The damage inflicted by the aggressor on the nation or community of nations must be lasting, grave, and certain;
2. All other means of putting an end to it must have been shown to be impractical or ineffective;
3. There must be serious prospects of success;
4. The use of arms must not produce evils and disorders

graver than the evil to be eliminated. The power of modern means of destruction weighs very heavily in evaluating this condition.

The national Conference of Catholic Bishops' 1983 statement had a
slightly different list, most importantly adding: 5) War must be
the last resort.[19] The *in bello* stipulations are less controversial: behavior in war must be discriminate (avoid harm to noncombatants) and proportional (use only an appropriate amount of force).

It is clear that Church leaders, pondering the carnage in two
World Wars and the threat of nuclear destruction, gave careful
thought to the fifth commandment. In the *Catechism*, the "non-
classical" prudential restrictions are logical and compelling consequences of the blunt two Latin words, *Non occides*, "Thou shalt not
kill"; the prudential restrictions on war may constitute a more
meaningful and effective statement on warfare than the three
"classic" standards Johnson and others endlessly commend. Indeed "classic" is a specious honorific: "Medieval" is more accurate
and less inflated.

These deontological standards have done little to reduce wartime fatalities. That may not even have been their function, as the
triad of sovereign authority, just cause and right intention often
served to endorse, not restrain, horrific slaughters. As the retired
colonel and legal historian G. I. A. Draper put it while comment-
ing on Johnson three decades ago:

> The trouble was that the just war doctrine had relatively little to say
> about conduct in warfare (*jus in bello*) beyond condemning perfidy....
> and the slaughter of women and children...The lack of restraint was
> compounded by the 14th and 15th-century ideas that the victorious
> Prince was waging a just war and, as the agent of God, punishing the
> defeated, as the devils in hell would punish them in the next
> world...The doctrine of the just war, religious or secular, has not had a
> fortunate impact upon conduct in warfare. The central vice of the me-
> dieval classic doctrine was that it oscillated between aggravation of the
> cruelties in war, because the victorious Prince as agent of God was
> punishing the unjust defeated, and a high level of artificiality that left it
> without an impact upon the content of the *jus in bello*.[20]

Frederick Hooker Russell concludes *The Just War in the Middle
Ages* on a similar note:

Provided that the cause was deemed just and the authority was competent, all means of prosecuting the war, including "aggressive" acts, were licit. Their approach was later to be termed the *ius ad bellum*, the right to war, whereas many modern commentators have concentrated, without notable success, on defining the limits on violence according to a *ius in bello*, the complex of rights and restrictions to be observed in wartime....Any assessments of just war theories are bound to be ambivalent, as were the theories themselves...Just war theory has had the dual purpose of restraining and justifying violence, essentially a self-contradictory exercise. Either the just war was a moral and religious doctrine, in which it was deprived of coercive but not normative force, or it was a legal concept that served as a cloak for statism. It remains an open question whether just war theories have limited more wars than they have encouraged.[21]

For the theological advocates of invading Iraq, the failure to limit war, the inattention to conduct, the terrible punishments for the defeated, and the "high level of artificiality" are inconsequential. What matters for them is the "pre-Westphalian" bliss of an era when state borders were at best advisory and invasion to set things right was an easy thing, or at least, easily embarked upon, and that is why their writings are filled with nostalgia. Elshtain is affronted by the modern "presumption of state sovereignty." Weigel regrets the loss of the "classic" just war tradition, and Johnson the "great loss" of just war "as it was." Lost in the verbiage was the likelihood that invading Iraq would increase, not reduce, the "hounding, torture, and murder" Elshtain claims to deplore.

It is not hard to see why "authority, cause and intention" did so little good. Consider, first, "right intention." Shakespeare's *Henry V* summarizes "right intention" with particular emphasis on the fate of those about to suffer, when he urges the Archbishop of Canterbury to speak with pure heart:

> And God forbid, my dear and faithful lord,
> That you should fashion, wrest, or bow your reading...
>
> For God doth know how many now in health
> Shall drop their blood in approbation
> Of what your reverence shall incite us to...

> Under this conjuration, speak, my lord;
> For we will hear, note and believe in heart
> That what you speak is in your conscience wash'd
> As pure as sin with baptism.[22]

It is hard to imagine a stronger and more effective plea for "right intention." But, the audience already knows, from the immediately preceding scene, that the Archbishop has already opted for war, with an ulterior motive: to distract the King from raising taxes on church lands. Henry hasn't a prayer of hearing speech "in …conscience wash'd / As pure as sin with baptism."

King Henry's speech conveys the deep emotional force of *intentio recta*, but Shakespeare's drama reveals the fragility and insincerity of proclamations of "good intent." In portraying his characters' multiple motives for war, Shakespeare also illustrates the difficulty of determining whether a state can even have "intentions." Such complexities may explain why "intention" is now absent from this section of the official Catholic *Catechism*.

"Just cause" is equally elusive. It was perhaps used to convince oneself that one's cause is just rather than the reverse: we regularly go into war convinced that "God is on our side," and so on. But the drafters of the *Catechism* may nevertheless have agreed that despite its antiquity "just cause" was not a good guide to just war. Pius XII, Murray reminds us, used this term only to describe self-defense against aggression.

"Sovereign authority," then, may be the only deontological cause that can be put to an empirical test. The Latin of the *Catechism* stresses "prudential judgment," the *prudens…iudicium* of "those who have responsibility for the common good." Supporters of the "classical" doctrine routinely ignore the weak or incompetent sovereigns whose names pepper the pages of history. In the very decade when the Apostle St. Paul was urging obedience to "God's servants for your good," the Roman historian Tacitus described one sorry emperor, Galba, as: *"Omnium consensu, capax imperii nisi imperasset."*[23] This passage could profitably be read alongside St. Paul's contemporary commendation of emperors. There are good reasons to restrict decisions about war to a sovereign authority, just as there are to respect the borders of a sovereign state: these are prerequisites of order. But that means only that sovereign authority is necessary, not that it is sufficient.

George Weigel and other critics of the U. S. Catholic bishops emphasize the *Catechism*'s acknowledgment of secular authority: perhaps they believe this prevents military second-guessing by common citizens, or, even worse, turbulent priests: "Responsible public authorities make the call" (George Weigel); "it is the responsibility of government leaders" (Richard John Neuhaus); "those public authorities who bear the immediate responsibility and who are closest to the facts of the case, have moral priority of place" (Michael Novak).

But, we can now ask who was more prudent and prescient: Weigel, Neuhaus, and Novak, or the American bishops, who publicly displayed their own *iudicium* in a September, 2002 letter to the President urging restraint against Iraq? ("We Urge You to Step Back from the Brink of War"):

> The use of force must have "serious prospects for success" and "must not produce evils and disorders graver than the evil to be eliminated" (Catechism, #2309). War against Iraq could have had unpredictable consequences not only for Iraq but for peace and stability elsewhere in the Middle East. Would preventive or preemptive force succeed in thwarting serious threats or, instead, provoke the very kind of attacks that it is intended to prevent? How would another war in Iraq impact the civilian population, in the short- and long-term? How many more innocent people would suffer and die, or be left without homes, without basic necessities, without work? Would the United States and the international community commit to the arduous, long-term task of ensuring a just peace or would a post-Saddam Iraq continue to be plagued by civil conflict and repression, and continue to serve as a destabilizing force in the region? Would the use of military force lead to wider conflict and instability? Would war against Iraq detract from our responsibility to help build a just and stable order in Afghanistan and undermine the broader coalition against terrorism?

Looking back in 2007 at the six months between the bishops' letter and the beginning of the invasion, we see why a democratic polity requires not just sovereign authority, but an informed and active citizenry. In these six months, the nation had ample opportunity to realize that *jus ad bellum*, "the right to make war," was dubious at best. The United Nations Monitoring, Verification and Inspection Commission, still at work, could find no evidence of weapons of mass destruction. News was emerging that American intelligence was unreliable, our planning for post-war Iraq was virtually nonexistent. Justice, proportionality, "last resort" and "prospects of success" seem not to have concerned the advisors of the American leadership in the least.

Some of the Catholic intellectuals who urged war now admit that they were sadly misled. Consider this statement:

> During the period leading up to the Iraq War, I was in regular conversation with the White House as part of what is called the Catholic Working Group. Karl Rove asked me to create this group after the 2000 election...We had many discussions with White House and Defense Department personnel about just war theory and the proposed invasion of Iraq. They were all well-versed in the basic principles...Our central concern...was not the issue of whether all other means had been exhausted -- we thought they had -- but whether there was an immediate danger to the United States...That's where WMDs came in...On one call with the White House we were all assured by a senior administration official that he had "absolute and certain proof" of WMDs. I asked if he could share the evidence with us. He said "no" but that we should "trust" him...Since this was someone I had known for a number of years in other circumstances, I had no reason not to believe him. (He, perhaps, had no reason not to believe the person who told him he had "absolute and certain proof" and so on.) We believed him.[24]

Deal Hudson appears to be the only member of the Catholic Working Group to have spoken in public about this matter, but Damon Linker, former editor of *First Things*, a conservative Catholic journal that promoted the invasion, joins Hudson in reporting manipulation by the White House:

> Writing days after the release of the final report on Saddam Hussein's weapons programs...Neuhaus chose to base his analysis not on the report itself but on a heavily redacted and deceptively interpreted version ... provided...by Karl Rove's White House deputy, Peter Wehner.[25]

Wehner's "deceptive interpretation" seems also to underlie George Weigel's essay in the April, 2007 issue of *First Things*, "Just War and Iraq Wars." Finally, Professor Elshtain, as late as 2006, maintained her faith in the "independent" government-sponsored briefings to which she was privileged:

> I am really struck by the different perceptions one gets depending on whether your exclusive source of information is the mass media – TV and newspapers – or whether you have some independent sources of information available to you, I am fortunate in that serving on the board of the National Endowment for Democracy, every three months we get briefings from people who are on the ground and are going back and forth to Baghdad. They describe the labour union effort, the women's groups, the rebuilding of schools, the rise of a free press.[26]

Elshtain's belief that the former Bush administration is more "independent" than the free press is touching indeed. "Right intention" seems, for her, Weigel and Neuhaus, to mean acquiescence toward a government, despite reports of governmental abuse of intelligence, incompetence and brutality. *Audi alteram partem*, "hear the other side," is always wise, and this group seems to have shut its ears to the other side, providing short-term support to the government, and doing long-term damage to an honorable tradition of thinking about warfare.

THE AUGUSTINIAN *CAVEAT PRAEEMPTOR*: PRUDENCE, PREEMPTION AND PREVENTION

Prudentia, in St. Augustine's *City of God*, is a human virtue. *Providentia*, "foresight," though etymologically identical (from *pro-* and *videre*, "to see ahead"), is associated only with the divinity and occasional patriarchs. Augustine speaks of prudence as a leadership trait that prevents "error from creeping in" (19.4): a haunting phrase when juxtaposed to the U. S. Secretary of State's admission of "thousands of tactical errors" in April 2006. Significantly, the demurrers that followed Secretary Condoleezza Rice's statement concerned the adjective, not the noun: errors in planning, strategy, and leadership were quickly added to "tactical" shortcomings. No one denied that errors occurred.

Prudence is weighty both in Augustine and in its one occurrence in the Catholic *Catechism*. Johnson, Weigel and others disparage it along with other non-deontological just war criteria. But abusing a cardinal virtue can backfire, and it has in this case: as we now see, "prudence" and "prudent judgment" would have prevented much damage in Iraq.

One argument for war against Iraq five years ago was that our invasion would be "defensive" or "preemptive." Robert George in December of 2002 spoke of Saddam as "a proven aggressor… in the process of equipping himself with the military means to carry out further aggression with impunity." The premise here (Saddam's "military means") was false, and George has written no more on this matter, but George Weigel continued to defend "defense" as late as April, 2007, insisting against all evidence that but for our invasion, Saddam Hussein "would have been back in the weapons-of-mass-destruction business in relatively short order." ("Would have" alerts readers that this is all fantasy. Weigel's enthusiasm for un-argued counterfactuals is the flip side of his aversion to embarrassing facts.)

"Preemption" and "prevention" are sometimes confused, although "preemptive" war (defense against a seemingly sure attack) is legally more defensible than "preventive" attacks (which seek to deny a potential threat the opportunity to grow). As Colin Gray notes, the two terms were speciously commingled in the run-up to the war, appearing more than twenty five times in the 2002 National Security Strategy (NSS) of the United States, in statements like this:

> [W]e will not hesitate to act alone, if necessary, to exercise our right of self-defense by acting preemptively against such terrorists, to prevent them from doing harm against our people and our country… To forestall or prevent such hostile acts by our adversaries, the United States will, if necessary, act preemptively.[27]

The two Bush National Security Strategies, of 2002 and 2006, never mention "prudence" and generally reject "deterrence." The 2002 NSS seems to have had little to do with objective analysis or good planning, and everything to do with promoting an invasion at the desired time. The lesson learned from this "preemptive" war may be summed up as, "let the preemptor beware": *Caveat Praeemptor.*

"THIS, TOO, IS THE FACE OF MODERN WAR": OUR ROMANCE WITH "PRECISION WEAPONS"

Even as body counts were soaring two years after the invasion, James Turner Johnson reported a breakthrough in an essay titled "Just War, As It Was and Is":

> The United States [has] channeled high technology in ways that allow war to be fought according to the actual principles of the just war *jus in bello*: this includes avoidance of direct, intended harm to noncombatants and avoidance of disproportionate harm in the use of otherwise justified means of war. The results, for those who care to look at them, are simply astonishing, especially by contrast to the level of destruction and the harm to noncombatant lives and property found, say, in carpet-bombing. This, too, is the face of modern war.

Johnson is responding to two documents he finds offensive: the American bishop's letter of 1983, *The Challenge of Peace*, and the fourth item in section 2309 of the *Catechism of the Catholic Church*, which mentioned "the power of modern means of destruction." George Weigel has also assailed the bishops' 1983 letter. Both men are aware, but neither bothers to mention, that the bishops wrote in a far different historical period, when nuclear winter threatened us all.

Does the *Catechism* merit such an attack, and should Professor Johnson be so complacent about modern weaponry? Bombing in modern warfare can indeed be precise. But precision attacks on water and electric supplies raise postwar death rates. Gulf War I, a 43-day conflict whose "surgical" features were widely admired, brought subsequent civilian deaths in the tens of thousands. The military strategist Colin Gray, no pacifist, notes the inevitable after-effect of bombing when he says, "There is much more to war than warfare."

A second consideration that troubled the bishops, if not their critics, is that many modern weapons are advanced not in their accuracy but only in their lethality. Readers will look in vain in Johnson's "authoritative" work for comments on fatality rates in Iraq, or on land mines or cluster bombs. *The Challenge of Peace* earned scorn from the right for its portrayal "of modern warfare as inherently grossly destructive, so much so that it could never be conducted morally or be an instrument of moral purpose" (Johnson in 2005). But Johnson's rosy scenarios about "limited war with restraint...fought in order to punish egregious aggression, to interdict terrible violence, to prevent further harm," or about "channeling high technology" are as remote from the reality of Iraq and Afghanistan as Cicero's theorizing was from Caesar's Gaul, or Paul's trust in the emperor from Titus' juggernaut on Jerusalem.

JUSTICE, MORALITY, AND EMPIRE

Augustine famously warned that even a just state, by seeking to impose itself on its neighbors and violate their sovereignty, may become less than just: "if justice is ignored," an emperor becomes equivalent to a "thief," a *latro*. In fact, the English philosopher, John Locke, would make the same point a millennium later. Augustine portrays Alexander the Great interrogating one such thief, a pirate:

> When the king asked him why he treated the ocean as an enemy, that fellow's frank and arrogant response was, "Why do you so treat the world? Because I act with one fragile boat, I am dubbed a 'thief': you, sailing with a huge fleet, are called 'Emperor.'[28]

Thus, this train of thought leads Augustine to compare great empire with grand larceny, *grande latrocinium*: "To impose wars on others...and to wear down and subdue peoples not harmful to oneself, out of a lust for rule, what can we call that but grand theft?" "Lust for rule" (*regni cupiditas*) links the thief's and the emperor's activity to a dominant Augustinian antinomy: "lust" (*voluptas, libido, cupiditas*) against "love" (*caritas*). "Passion for rule" (*libido dominandi*) occurs at least a dozen times in *The City of God*, and Augustine reminds us (3.14) that the phrase comes from the Roman historian Sallust's characterization of Rome itself. On inspection, we find that it almost always refers to ancient Rome and its thirst for dominance.

At a time when "American primacy" or "unipolarity" increasingly prompts comparisons with ancient Rome, Augustine's usage bears noting. Great emperors can resemble pirates, and imperialism, brigandage, especially if city or leader is poisoned by

"lust." This warning seems to be lost on Elshtain and other proponents of intervention. American "humanitarian reasons" do not
exclude acquisitive drives, for instance the desire for oil, or for
long-term military bases. This is happening in Iraq, Somalia,
Kosovo, and Afghanistan, among other countries.

Many of the so-called contemporary "Augustinians" ignore
key elements of St. Augustine's own moral message. The language
of *The City of God* reveals a deep sensitivity to the moral and
structural temptations facing an imperial power. Consider, for instance, the unsettling use of interrogatives. Does any ancient
author pose as many pointed questions as Augustine? Book 4 of
The City of God has over two hundred, and Book 19 nearly one
hundred. Augustine questions: "With justice removed, what are
empires but massive larcenies?" "What are larcenies but tiny empires?" and "To bring wars on neighbors and…merely from lust
to rule, to wear down and subjugate inoffensive peoples, what is
this but great theft?"

Under these probing questions, formulas like "humanitarian
intervention" lose their allure, and we have a terrible need for
such questions in our new era of "telescopic philanthropy" and
human rights. Television can make brutality seem immediate, but
struggles to convey its cause, and to offer effective solutions. A
large number of Americans, after all, shared Elshtain's and Weigel's enthusiasm for invading Iraq. Americans were aware of suffering populations around the world, and clearly wanted to do
something. The International Commission on Intervention and
State Sovereignty reflected this desire in *The Responsibility to Protect* in December, 2001: "Responsibility to protect" seemed on its
way to becoming a new universal, with the invasion of Iraq at the
crest of this movement. The dark side of humanitarian intervention discussed by Anne Orford and others – the frequently dirty
hands of intervenors, and their tendency to manipulate intervention in their own interest – was less evident.

That said, it has to be added that some of Augustine's asser-
tions could be as damaging as his questions were beneficial. One
lasting and troubling legacy of Augustine, for instance, is the notion that justice lies on one side only. St. Augustine gives the impression that war does not occur, or should not occur, between

two equally justified parties; he uses words like "iniquity" and "evil" so often that readers may become convinced of their own rectitude and of opponents' membership in an axis of evil, as "wrongdoers" or "evildoers": especially since the judge and the ruler are identical: the leader, decision-maker, or "decider" reports to none other than himself and his God. Without an outside authority to judge our decisions, we risk constant error.

CONCLUSION: CAN JUST WAR THEORY BE SAVED?

The current debate over "just wars" reveals more than its participants intended. On the one hand, Elshtain, Johnson, Weigel and others seek to revive the "tradition." But their advocacy forces us to ask, with Draper and Russell, just why resuscitation is deserved? If traditional just war theory has had a positive effect on the behavior of "earthly cities," if the theory has had a genuinely regulative rather than a permissive function, the theorists discussed in this essay have assiduously ignored these outcomes. Johnson and Elstain's ode to "precision weapons," their neglect of the evils of land mines and cluster bombs and blind eye to American responsibility for Darfur-like fatalities do not speak well for this "tradition."

In short, the Thomistic triad risks appearing elegant but vaporous. "Just cause," "sovereign authority" and "right intention" appear too malleable to serve as standards of state behavior. The current "prudential" positions of the American bishops and of the *Catechism*, not to mention Popes John Paul II and Benedict XVI, assess what war does and what states can do more realistically, and they provide more hope for the future. War kills innocents not only on the battlefield but from malnutrition, filthy water, and other after-effects: as we see in Iraq, it can easily "produce evils and disorders graver than the evil to be eliminated." For this and other reasons, it must remain a last resort, a response to aggression when all other means are exhausted and when success is clearly possible.

But even if the "traditional" justifications for war seem dangerously flimsy, they retain substantial force as a set of aspirations. Who would not want a world in which sovereigns take their authority seriously, in which justice is a serious and not simply rhetorical standard, in which advocates of war rigorously scrutinize their "intentions"? Even if such a goal is hopelessly idealistic, this ideal may have some positive effect on our consciences. But that is true too of the "aspirations" of the pacifists who are regularly dismissed by just war theorists. From this point of view, both pacifism and traditional "just war" remain remote, "absurd" ...and powerful, even if they can be approached only asymptotically.

Notes

[1] Cf. the American Catholic bishops' Pastoral Letter on War (1983) in the revised *Catechism*, which insists that military action have "serious prospects of success." It also mentions modern weapons that bring new horrors (*modernorum destructionis mediorum potentia*) and warns against "graver woes than the evil under attack," (section 2309, composed under John Paul II). Complaints: Jean Bethke Elshtain, "International Justice as Equal Regard and the Use of Force," *Ethics & International Affairs* vol. 17 no. 2 (2003), 63-75; Elshtain's "Interview with Neil Conan," *Talk of the Nation*, National Public Radio (April 30, 2003); James Turner Johnson, "Just War, As It Was and Is," *First Things* 149 (January 2005), 14-24; George Weigel, "Moral Clarity in a Time of War," *First Things* 129 (January 2003), 25.

[2] Cicero, *De Officiis* 1.35; Plutarch, *Caesar* 15.

[3] St. Paul, *Romans* 13.1-2 RSV.

[4] Cf. *Romans* 15:25, *Acts* 21-28.

[5] *Romans* 13:9-10.

[6] Michael Novak, "'Asymmetrical Warfare' & Just War: A Moral Obligation," *National Review Online*, (February 10, 2003). Also: http://www.nationalreview.com/articles/205864/asymmetrical-warfare-just-war/michael-novak (Accessed March 24, 2010); Neuhaus in *First Things* (February 1, 2006) and earlier.

[7] Augustine, *City of God* XIX.19.

[8] *Summa Theologiae* II–II, 40.1.

[9] Cf. Elshtain, "Interview with Neil Conan."

[10] Leslie H. Gelb and Justine A. Rosenthal, "The Rise of Ethics in Foreign Policy: Reaching a Values Consensus," *Foreign Affairs* vol. 82 no. 3 (May/June 2003), 2-7.

[11] Edward J. Mills and Frederick M. Burkle. Jr., "Interference, Intimidation, and Measuring Mortality in War," *The Lancet* 373 (April 18, 2009), 1320-1322. Cf. also Gilbert Burnham, Riyadh Lafta, Shannon Doocy and Les Roberts, "Mortality

after the 2003 Invasion of Iraq: A Cross-Sectional Cluster Sample Survey," *The Lancet* 368 (October 21, 2006), 1421-1428.

[12] Anne Orford, *Reading Humanitarian Intervention: Human Rights and the Use of Force in International Law* (Cambridge: Cambridge University Press, 2005), 158-185; Anne Orford, "Locating the International: Military and Monetary Interventions after the Cold War," *Harvard International Law Journal* 38 (Spring 1997) 443 – 485.

[13] Cf. Elshtain, "The Responsibility of Nations: A Moral Case for Coercive Justice," *Daedalus* 132 (Winter 2003), 64-72. Other authors sharing her low opinion of the Peace of Westphalia include George Weigel, "Moral Clarity in a Time of War," *First Things* 128 (January 2003), 20-27 (who acknowledged "will argue that this violates the principle of sovereignty and risks a global descent into chaos") and James Turner Johnson, "The Just War Idea: The State of the Question," *Social Philosophy and Policy* 23 (2006), 23, 167-195 and "Just War, As It Was and Is," *First Things* 149 (January 2005), 14-24 and elsewhere, Kenneth R. Himes, "Intervention, Just War, and U.S. National Security," *Theological Studies* vol. 65 (March 2004).

[14] Daniel Philpott, "The Challenge Of September 11 To Secularism In International Relations," *World Politics* vol. 55 no. 1 (2002), 74.

[15] T. M. Parker, "St. Augustine and the Conception of Unitary Sovereignty," *Augustinus Magister: Congrès International Augustinien,* vol. 2 (Paris: Études Augustiniennes, 1955), 951-955.

[16] Augustine, *On Christian Doctrine* III.10.16.

[17] "The Realists and Saint Augustine: Skepticism, Psychology, and Moral Action in International Relations Thought," *International Studies Quarterly*, vol. 36, no. 4 (December 1992), 416.

[18] John Courtney Murray, *We Hold These Truths* (Garden City: Doubleday Image, 1964), 245 cited in Kenneth Himes, "Intervention, Just War, and U.S. National Security," *Theological Studies* vol. 65, no.1 (2004).

[19] National Conference of Catholic Bishops, *The Challenge of Peace: God's Promise and Our Response* (Washington: United States Catholic Conference, 1983).

[20] G.I.A.D. Draper, review of James Turner Johnson, *Ideology, Reason, and the Limitations of War: Religious and Secular Concepts*, in *Yale Law Journal* vol. 86 no. 2 (1976), 376.

[21] Frederick Hooker Russell, *The Just War in the Middle Ages* (Cambridge: Cambridge University Press, 1975), 308.

[22] Shakespeare, *Henry V*, 1.2.

[23] Tacitus, *Histories* 1.49: "In the opinion of all, capable of rule – if only he had not ruled."

[24] "Deal Hudson's WMD's and the Iraq War," April 17, 2007 http://catholicjustwar.blogspot.com/2007_04_01_archive.html (accessed June 22, 2007).

[25] Damon Linker, *The Theocons: Secular America Under Siege* (New York: Doubleday, 2006), 137.

[26] "Just War, Humanitarian Intervention and Equal Regard: An Interview with Jean Bethke Elshtain, in Global Politics After 9/11" *The Democratiya Interviews*, ed. and intro. by Alan Johnson, http://fpc.org.uk/fsblob/901.pdf (accessed March 24, 2011).

[27] "We will not hesitate" can be found in the 2002 National Security Strategy at: http://georgewbush-whitehouse.archives.gov/nsc/nss/2002/print/nss3.html (accessed March 24, 2011). Cf. the long discussion devoted to this statement by strategist Colin S. Gray, "The Implications of Preemptive and Preventive War Doctrines: A Reconsideration," *US Army, Strategic Studies Institute* (July 2007) http://www.dtic.mil/cgibin/GetTRDoc?AD=ADA470484&Location=U2&doc=Get TRDoc.pdf (accessed March 24, 2011).

[28] Augustine, *The City of God* IV.4.

Editors, Contributors and Symposium Participants

Dieter Blumenwitz is Professor of International Law at the Ukrainian Free University in Munich, Germany.

John D. Caputo is Thomas J. Watson Professor of Religion and the Humanities at Syracuse University and David R. Cook Chair Emeritus of Philosophy at Villanova University. Professor Caputo is a renowned philosopher and distinguished authority on Heidegger, deconstruction and postmodern philosophy. Author and editor of over seventeen books and innumerable articles, his recent works include *The Weakness of God: A Theology of the Event* (2006), *Philosophy and Theology* (2006) and *Augustine and Postmodernism: Confessions and Circumfession* (2005).

Rev. Craig J. N. de Paulo is a professor of philosophy and theology at Gwynedd Mercy College. A distinguished historian of philosophy and Augustine scholar, Professor de Paulo has published numerous books, including *The Influence of Augustine on Heidegger: The Emergence of an Augustinian Phenomenology, Ambiguity in the Western Mind, Being and Conversion*, and recently *Confessions of Love: The Ambiguities of Greek Eros and Latin Caritas*. He holds a Ph.D and Ph.L. in philosophy from the Pontifical Gregorian University in Rome.

His Eminence, Avery Cardinal Dulles, S. J. held the Laurence J. McGinley Professor of Religion and Society at Fordham University until his recent passing. Cardinal Dulles held a doctorate in theology from the Pontifical Gregorian University in Rome, and he was one of the most prominent Catholic theologians of our time.

Joseph H. Hagan is President Emeritus of Assumption College in Worcester, Massachusetts. Currently, he serves as Chairman of the Board of Trustees at John Cabot University in Rome, Italy.

John M. Haas is President of the National Catholic Bio-Ethics Center in Philadelphia and formerly the John Cardinal Krol Chair of Moral Theology at St. Charles Borromeo Seminary also in Philadelphia.

Jack Jacobs is a retired Colonel in the United States Army and currently Military Analyst for MSNBC. As a recipient of the Medal of Honor, he is one of the most highly decorated retired officers in the United States.

Brian Kane is Chair and Professor of Philosophy and Theology at De Sales University in Center Valley, Pennsylvania.

Joseph Margolis is Laura H. Carnell Professor of Philosophy at Temple University in Philadelphia, Pennsylvania. Professor Margolis is one of the most accomplished and renowned philosophers in the United States. Author and editor of over forty books and countless articles, his recent works include *The Philosophical Challenge of September 11* (2003) and *The Unraveling of Scientism: American Philosophy at the End of the Twentieth Century* (2003).

George J. Marlin is a conservative political writer and columnist and former Executive Director of the Port Authority of New York and New Jersey. Mr. Marlin is the author and editor of several books on American politics and literature. He is currently the Chairman of the Philadelphia Trust Company.

Hon. Thomas Melady is former U.S. Ambassador to the Holy See (1989-1993), to Uganda (1972-1974) and to Burundi (1969-1972). He is currently Senior Diplomat-in-Residence at the World Institute of Politics in Washington, D.C. Ambassador Melady holds a Ph.D. in political science from the Catholic University of America.

Patrick A. Messina is Assistant Professor of Philosophy at Gwynedd Mercy College. He co-edited *Ambiguity in the Western Mind* and *Confessions of Love: The Ambiguities of Greek Eros and Latin Caritas*. He holds a Ph.D. from the Pontifical Athenaeum of St. Anselm and a Ph.L. from the Pontifical Gregorian University in Rome.

His Excellency, The Most Rev. Edwin F. O'Brien is Archbishop of Baltimore and Archbishop Emeritus of the U. S. Military Archdiocese. Holding a doctorate in theology from the Pontifical University of St. Thomas Aquinas, the *Angelicum*, in Rome, Archbishop O'Brien is Rector Emeritus of the North American College in Rome and Rector Emeritus of St. Joseph's Seminary, Dunwoody, in New York.

His Eminence, The Most Rev. Seán Cardinal O'Malley, O.F.M. Cap. is Archbishop of Boston. Cardinal O'Malley holds a Ph.D. in Spanish and Portuguese Literature from Catholic University of America, where he was a professor from 1969 to 1973.

Rev. Roland J. Teske, S.J. is the Donald J. Schuenke Chair of Philosophy at Marquette University. Father Teske is a renowned Medievalist and Augustine scholar, having translated several of his works into English and published over thirty books and countless articles.

Daniel P. Tompkins is Associate Professor Emeritus of Greek and Roman Classics at Temple University. He holds a Ph.D. from Yale University.

Frederick Van Fleteren is Professor of Philosophy at La Salle University in Philadelphia. Professor Van Fleteren is an eminent scholar in Augustine and the Augustinian tradition and has published numerous books and articles.